D0420719

The Road to Europe

Irish Attitudes 1948-61

Miriam Hederman

Institute of Public Administration

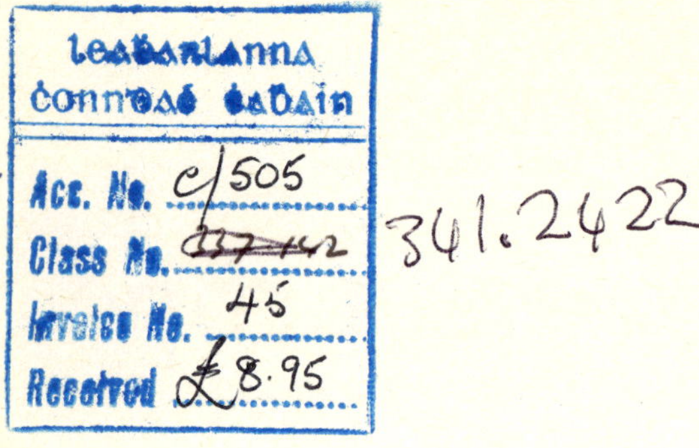

First published 1983

by the Institute of Public Administration
57-61 Lansdowne Road, Dublin 4, Ireland

British Library Cataloguing in Publication Data

Hederman, Miriam
The Road to Europe
1. European federation 2. European Economic Community—Economic integration
I. Title
337.1'42 HC241.2

ISBN 0 906980 28 3

Design by Della Varilly
Typeset and printed by Cahill Printers Limited, Dublin 3

Contents

Preface

This study was undertaken to place on record the development of thought and policy on European integration in Ireland during a period popularly considered to be largely barren of any European relevance. It was inspired by memories of my own involvement in the European Youth Campaign and European Movement in the fifties, and of the personalities who played their parts on the Irish and European stage. It was originally a thesis, because in that way it could serve as a source for those who wished to explore the hitherto uncharted material of the period, not only on European integration but on the many metamorphoses undergone by sections of Irish society which affected Irish-European relations. It was made possible by the co-operation of many people who were influential during that time or immediately afterwards. I would therefore like to acknowledge the great help I received from all those who are listed as having given interviews or access to documents, or prepared memoranda for the purpose of this book. There were others who were anxious to assist but had no records extant – they saved many hours of fruitless search and thereby made the work easier.

The second group of people to whom a debt of gratitude is due are those who helped the work in general: the Library staff in Trinity College; the Assistant Director of the College of Europe, Bruges, Dr M. Paklons; the Secretary General of the International European Movement, M. R. van Schendal; the Chief Archivist of the Council of Europe, Mr J. Keith Bishop; Professor Walter Lipgens and three post-graduate students at the European University Institute – Messrs Christian Huber, Alan Hick and Dermot Keogh;

Mr Denis Corboy and Mr Tim Kelly of the EEC Commission Office in Dublin, M. Joseph Sans, Mesdames Fausta Deshormes and Jacqueline Lastenousse of the EEC Commission in Brussels; the staff of the Library in the Institute of Public Administration; the Officials of the Department of Foreign Affairs, in particular Miss Ann Barrington who made available the records of *Éire/Ireland;* the Chief Librarian of RTE, Mr Diarmuid Breathnach and his assistants; the staffs of many private, state-sponsored, professional and trade union organisations who facilitated my searches in the records of their organisations; those who patiently read early drafts of individual chapters and made constructive criticisms, particularly Dr Charles McCarthy, Dr Ronan Fanning, Dr T. K. Whitaker and Mr E. G. Thompson. A particular tribute should be paid to my supervisor, Dr Patrick Keatinge, who read the many drafts which emerged between the first, tentative outline and the reorganised thesis.

The financial assistance of the Commission of the European Communities towards the publication of this study in book form is gratefully acknowledged.

Thanks are also due to Mrs Ann McLernon who transformed the heavily amended text into its final, well presented and typed format. And a last acknowledgment must be made to my husband, Bill, who spliced the infinitives and corrected the more obvious eccentricities of syntax and style.

Introduction

Most countries of Western Europe boast a considerable volume of material devoted to analysis and discussion of the political and economic aftermath of the 1939-45 War and the growth of the phenomenon of voluntary integration of nation-states. It is considered not only natural but essential for an understanding of the past and present policies of these countries.

The situation in Ireland is somewhat different. The manner in which Irish public opinion, government and pressure groups developed their attitudes between the country's first exposure to the idea of European integration and its decision to apply for full membership of the European Communities in 1961 has not been charted. Observers might be forgiven for believing that the idea sprang, Minerva like, from the brain of Seán Lemass. This work is an attempt to describe the processes which occurred, to relate developments in Ireland with those in Europe and to point to some of the more interesting changes in Irish life during the period. The European Congress of The Hague is the clearest date with which to begin a study of the evolutionary process which took place. Since 1948 was also the date of the election of the first Inter-Party or Coalition government it makes a natural landmark in national and international politics. The closing date imposes itself equally rationally. Apart from the change brought about by the actual application for membership in 1961, records are more plentiful and there is more material extant from that date onwards, so the urgent need to harvest the dwindling crop of records and recollections which survive from the earlier period does not apply.

Material

The material has been gathered from four main sources:

1. Unpublished files and documents, coming mainly from the archives of the College of Europe in Bruges, and of the Council of Europe in Strasbourg, and of people and organisations involved at the period e.g. Seán MacBride, Comhairle le Leas Oige, etc.

2. Recordings and publicity material from Radio Éireann archives.

3. Published material: newspapers, periodicals, Official Publications (Dáil Reports, Council of Europe Reports, etc.); newsletters and periodicals for internal circulation e.g. Reports of Institute of Bankers, Federation of Irish Manufacturers, etc.; other studies relevant to the period.

4. People who had been involved: e.g. Lady Wicklow, Emile Noel, Seán Healy, Seán MacBride, etc.

Dealing with the material posed some serious difficulties. The first and most obvious place to look for clues to government policy and civil service advice is naturally the records of government departments. A courteous but unrewarding correspondence with the Department of Foreign Affairs revealed that while an answer given by the Tánaiste and Minister for the Public Service in reply to a Dáil Question on 15 December 1977 might have indicated to the optimistic that legislation would soon be on its way[1] to enable serious students to have access to state papers, there has been no change since that date and the files of the departments are not available.

It has therefore been necessary to go ahead without this very important source, particularly for papers relating to membership of the Organisation for Economic Co-operation, the Council of Europe and the European Community.

A second, somewhat surprising difficulty occurred in connection with reactions from Northern Ireland. It was not possible to find in Dublin copies of Belfast daily newspapers of the period under review. Since it was not possible, despite several visits to Belfast during the course of preparation for this study, to wade through more than a fraction of the material, and since such efforts yielded little or nothing of relevance, the Northern papers had to be ignored.

The third problem arose from the manner in which relevant material had either disappeared or been destroyed. The late Donal O'Sullivan, the first chairman of the Irish Council of the European Movement and a man known to make and keep notes on his various activities must have kept records of the manner in which he eventually set up the Irish Council. Yet despite the co-operation of his widow, Mrs Jennie O'Sullivan, and of the Department of Education (in whose keeping his work on Irish traditional music and other subjects has been left) and the help of University College Dublin and Dublin University, in both of which he worked, it has been impossible to trace these particular records. As far as many other individuals and groups are concerned, the material has simply been destroyed, or never kept.

Requests for access to personal papers and files, relating to events of thirty years ago, were most generously answered by the people involved. (One of the few exceptions was the official national students' organisation.) This was the first approach the majority had received to help reconstruct a largely ignored era of recent Irish history and they unanimously favoured the idea of saving such material as had survived for the benefit of future students.

Lest it be feared that the results of all searches were negative it should be noted that the 'finds' of the archives of the College of Europe in Bruges, in which the author was only the second researcher and the first to examine those relating to Ireland, represent a vein of information which it is hoped others will mine more deeply. Furthermore, the other unpublished material is well worth preserving and exploring further. Since this work was started records of the Irish Council of the European Movement have been collected and are now lodged, with other documents, in the archives section of the Office of the Commission of the European Community in Dublin.

The importance of the reconstructed material from Radio Éireann should not be overlooked nor the contributions, albeit necessarily anonymous, from members of the civil service. In the absence of the official files of the Department of Foreign Affairs, recourse was had to the Department's Bulletin which revealed aspects which the Department officials wished to emphasise, thus unfolding their attitudes in a context different from but perhaps as important as those contained in memoranda or confidential reports. Finally, the effort to relate European developments to those taking place in Ireland, even when made through material already published, has thrown new light on the Irish scene. The Irish stage has been closely studied when it was the centre of violence. The story of its more peaceful transformations has received less attention.

Methodology

The study has been divided into two parts.

Chapters One to Five deal with the gradual unfolding of events, with public reaction to them and also with the relationship between developments in Europe and those in Ireland from 1948-1961. The chief actors in this section are the politicians.

Chapters Six to Ten give more detailed information on the *means* by which attitudes were formed and reflected and the groups (or 'élites') which were involved, ending with the general picture of the period which has emerged.

'Élite' is often popularly used to describe persons who enjoy superior social status. In this study it is used to describe those whose role is to influence or even control the society in which they operate.

If 'élites' are fairly straightforward, other aspects are not. Methodological difficulties arise in handling the material itself. The first is the obvious one of terminology. Human attitudes, although they may be studied with ethical neutrality, are not themselves neutral and account must be taken of terms which change their connotation in time and place and according to the people using them. 'Loyalty', 'patriotism', 'co-operation', 'nationalism', 'integration' itself and many, many others change their emphasis according to their context. The social and political scientists have partially overcome this difficulty by developing a new language which may well be impartial and original but is used and understood only by its creators. I have used the terms which were in vogue during the period and tried to describe their context sufficiently clearly so that the reader can evaluate their meaning to those who actually used them.

The second problem is one of bias. To determine the connections between different sets of variables one must select some and discard others. Some are studied because they can be ascertained and therefore gain a posthumous importance through the survival of their records, an importance they may not have deserved at the time. Even initial comparisons require a value judgment and some aspects of Irish life have, in this study, been underlined because they appear to have been ignored elsewhere.

A comparison with international studies on the integrative process which took place in Western Europe after the war indicates that these two difficulties have also arisen, even in the most elevated academic circles. 'Federalism', 'functionalism', 'spill-over', 'internationalism', 'supranational', even 'community', are terms with varying meanings. In an effort to attain precision, eminent authors, including E. B. Haas, Morton Kaplan, A. Etizioni, David Mitrany and Leon Lindberg have defined, redefined and invented words for subsequent use. This is possibly justified in academic work which involves pushing analyses into new frontiers and synthesising the apparently chaotic and haphazard evolution of political life. It seems to me pretentious (although tempting) to coin a term to describe, for example, the attitudes of Irish political leaders, both in and out of office, to European integration. But because it has been necessary, on occasion, to use at least three of these terms in connection with the Irish situation the following broad definitions have been adopted. 'Functionalism' is taken to mean the non-political approach to international co-operation, founded on the belief that enlightened self-interest and the mere fact of working together to solve common problems will eliminate most areas of conflict between nations and peoples. It is essentially pragmatic. 'Federalism' is understood as a method of achieving political union between separate states while, at the same time, diffusing power so that it is exercised at the most appropriate level (local, regional, national and federal). Such a view assumes the existence of conflict in society and seeks to give as much expression as possible to different ethnic, linguistic, geographical and economic regions while ensuring adequate co-ordination and development of the whole. 'Neo-functionalism' was developed largely to explain what had happened in the context of European developments and to provide an acceptable middle way for those who found functionalism too utilitarian and federalism too doctrinaire. It could be roughly described as the belief that integration in certain areas can co-exist with the life of sovereign nation states but that the existence of such integration, and the organisation which controls it, will bring about an expansion of integration and the joint activity will be larger than the sum of the original activities. It has been of some comfort to discover that Haas admits, 'most neo-functionalists have not explicitly recognised . . . the crucial question of whether . . . this incremental style is not "foreseen" and manipulated by certain heroic actors (Jean Monnet, Siccho Mansholt, Walter Hallstein, Paul Prebisch) – and eventually checked by certain equally prescient national actors (Charles de Gaulle).'[2] The author of this work would push this further and claim that not only does reality insist that the instincts and public attitudes of people such as MacBride, de Valera, Lemass, have an effect on the community in which they play their leading roles, but that other lesser though important players introduce an important if non-quantifiable element into the development of public opinion and the change in attitudes which are the marks of a living society.

The treatment of the material has been straightforward. The chronological section, Chapters One to Five, begins with the post-war situation in Ireland and relates it to the larger continental scene. The study proper begins in Chapter Two with the Congress of The Hague and continues with developments on the European mainland and Irish reactions to them. While 'home' attitudes were shaped by matters which loomed large on the domestic horizon (such as emigration, the IRA activity, the partition of the country, and other questions peculiar to Ireland) it is evident that Irish problems did not push European policies in any particular direction, nor did Irish leaders make any significant contribution to the political debate about the shape, direction and pace of European integration.

These first five chapters reveal a sub-plot concerning the economic situation of the country which varied between 'bad' and 'worse' when compared to European progress for the greater part of the period covered. This became so patent (even as a recurring excuse for inability to attend conferences abroad or as reasons for foregoing a role in international organisations) that there was a danger that references to the economic straits of the period would become a constant lament.

The second part of the work deals, in as much depth as available source material will allow, with the two most important forces affecting 'attitudes': (1) the media; and (2) the groups and élites who formed the leadership of the period. Without being a slave to McLuhanism, it is possible to emphasise the importance of the changes in the *means* of communication, both in the context of the existing media of press and radio, and of the addition of television, to the formation of public opinion during the years under review.

The élites, actors and pressure groups deserve special attention, even though many of them have figured also in the chronological chapters. Some have been singled out because of their particular role in taking sides on whether or not Ireland should take any part in an integrated Europe. It has been necessary in the section dealing with the élites to rely heavily on the personal recollections of those involved at the time. Every effort has been made to compare reminiscences with each other and to check the spoken word with the available written records, such as they are.

The concluding chapter, while unorthodox, seemed the only logical close to a study which raised as many questions as it answered.

Part One

Ireland in the Post-War World

Four features distinguish Ireland from its European neighbours in the immediate post-war era.

The first is its neutrality and the effect this had both on Irish prestige abroad and on the Irish self-image at home. There were marked differences between Ireland's neutrality and that of other European countries, so the Irish brand needs at least a little explanation.

The second feature was the existence of 'Northern Ireland' as a part of the United Kingdom, on the island of Ireland. This complicated and coloured national policies, relations with Britain and, eventually, international and European relations.

Third, there was a continuing mass emigration which affected the potential for social and economic progress and left its mark on the cultural and psychological development of the people.

Fourth, there was the Irish view of the outside world, strongly influenced by Irish myth and history – which were often indistinguishable – and underpinned by Irish nationalism.

Thousands of Irishmen fought in the Allied forces during the Second World War and thousands more men and women worked in the factories and hospitals and throughout the United Kingdom in jobs described as vital to the war effort. The vast majority of the Irish people saw no contradiction between personally fighting for 'England' against Germany or earning their living as part of the war-machine, and supporting a policy of neutrality 'at home'. A small group still considered England's difficulty as Ireland's opportunity. The IRA leaders had contacts in

Germany, indeed two of them, Sean Russell and Frank Ryan, were in Germany when war broke out. However, IRA raids on the border between the twenty-six counties and the six counties of Northern Ireland which were still part of the United Kingdom, received little or no support throughout the country as a whole. Had the Allies decided to invade Ireland, however, there is no doubt that resistance would have been fierce, bitter and universal. Neutrality, even on sufferance, suited both sides.

And yet Edouard Hempel, the German Minister in Dublin during the war, was under no illusion as to where Irish sympathies lay. Neutrality 'visibly strengthened Irish national self-consciousness' but there was 'widespread aversion to present-day Germany, especially for religious reasons'.[1]

From its very creation the unit of Northern Ireland had been a problem child. It was called Ulster but it included only six of the nine counties of the ancient province of Ulster. As a prominent Ulsterman, John Cole, has described it:

> From the start the Ulster state has been a deeply divided community. For while a majority of its people, the Protestants, would have been happy to continue under direct rule from Westminster, the one-third of the population that was Catholic wanted to be part of the Irish Free State. The creation of the Ulster Parliament and Government was an attempt to reconcile the irreconcilable, to bundle both sets of aspirations into a shabby compromise: the Protestants would accept it as maintaining their position within the Union; the Catholics would hope that the Parliaments in Dublin and Belfast would eventually create the projected Council of Ireland (a body which never progressed beyond the pages of the 1920 Government of Ireland Act).[2]

This partition of the island has had its influence on attitudes of both North and South to the outside world; though it has had less impact on successive Irish governments' attitudes to European integration than to other aspects of their foreign policy, it cannot be ignored as a fact of Irish political life.

The social, political, economic and cultural climate of the immediate postwar period has left a disagreeable image in the national memory. But perhaps the image of a timid, truculent, narrow-minded and philistine people owes more to the irritation of angry men and women of letters than to social historians. The Censorship of Publications Act alienated a generation of Irish writers and, as the chieftains of Ireland had learned to their cost centuries earlier, it does not pay to irritate the bards.

However, Seán Ó Faoláin, usually the scourge of the establishment, writes sympathetically of the transition from peasant to townsman and the trauma of assuming responsibility for their own fate which the Irish had to cope with after the independence of the state.

> They (the peasants) did not prosper. But they held on with a tenacity that is the most moving and astounding spectacle in the whole Irish story . . . through generation after generation, starving not by thousands but millions, falling into the earth like the dung of cattle, weeping and cursing as they slaved, patient alike under the indifference of God and of their masters, they clung to their wretched bits of land as it were by their bleeding finger-nails . . . so that even when we are most bored, or utterly sick of the extravagances and crudities of Irish nationalism, we have to sympathise, and we try again to understand. I suppose that even the most urbane and civil Irishman could, and will if he is wise, acknowledge that there is in him a vestigial angel or devil that, in propitious circumstances, is capable of turning him into a hero or a savage at the memory of what his fathers endured.[3]

One of the preoccupations of Ireland, not shared by her European neighbours, was the effect of emigration on her ability to make progress.

The most authentic statement of official concern in the period under review is the Report of the Commission appointed in April 1948 by the Minister for Social Welfare to study 'Irish Population Problems' which was published in July 1954. The majority report, signed by twenty-two of the members of the Commission (minority reports being made by Dr Cornelius Lucey, Bishop of Cork and James Meenan, Lecturer in Economics, University College, Dublin) listed the undesirable consequences of the marriage pattern then prevalent in Ireland and adduced the following reasons for it: 'low agricultural income, under-development in production other than agriculture; the desire for improved material standards; the late ages at which farmers' sons inherit farms and the uncertainty as to succession to the farm on the death of the farmer'.

The consequences of emigration, however, were far-reaching, and the factors which affected it complex. Not only did emigration deprive the country of part of its potentially productive man-power (although the Commission discounted the view that it is 'the best' who emigrate) but, by reducing population pressure on resources at home, it led to a too-easy acquiescence in conditions of under-development.

Emigration affected Irish economic, social and cultural life. It was a factor, moreover, which separated Ireland from Europe because emigration was limited to English-speaking countries. Both those who contemplated emigration and those who kept in touch (financially or otherwise) with emigrants had no reason to make any contact with the 'mainland' of Europe.

The apparent timidity of Irish leaders when faced with the possibility of initiating some revolutionary economic or social programme must be taken as a contrast to some of the revolutionary steps of the pre-war era. As far as lack of courage in other respects was concerned, probably a desire to keep out the more excessive sexual crudities fostered by western capitalism, rather than any failure of nerve, made certain eminent figures acquiesce in a system of censorship which they would otherwise have considered excessive and even ridiculous.

The prevailing Irish attitude to Europe was nostalgic, warm and idealised. (Europe here must be understood to exclude Great Britain and the USSR; the former because the relationship had been so prolonged and emotional that it was on quite a different footing; the USSR because it was, for the great majority of the Irish people a world apart: communist, vast, terrible and largely unknown.) As far as 'greater Europe' was concerned popular views might be summed up as follows: Italy was a friendly country, the Italians sympathetic (though politically misguided perhaps) and Rome, as the seat of the Vatican, assumed to be an ally; France was admired for her culture and flair and commemorated in song and poetry for acts of friendship throughout the centuries that had long since been forgotten by the French (and which were inspired more by the political quarrels of the time than any great love of the wild Irish); Denmark, Holland and Belgium were regarded with some envy as small countries which had made their mark on the world (their strong co-operative movements and flourishing agriculture were constantly used as examples in the Irish countryside); Germany provoked more fear than affection but Austria retained its aura of music and glory and romance, mainly perhaps because so few Irish had managed to travel there; the Spanish civil war had had repercussions in Irish political life[4] so the picture was probably a little closer to the reality than that of Portugal, for example, which was associated with Our Lady of Fatima, a somewhat unworldly image; Poland was always regarded with great sympathy, the analogy of repression and invasion acting as a bond; Turkey was looked on more as part of Asia Minor than of Europe but Greece floated in the after-glow of a smattering of classical education administered to most boys and a few girls in Irish secondary schools; the countries of Central Europe caused some confusion because of their changing fates but, again, as with Poland, were regarded with sympathy; Switzerland was a land apart, well-ordered, secure, prosperous and aloof.

The Irish had more family ties with the United States than with continental Europe, but they saw themselves as Europeans, part of the old world, and if their bird's eye view of European countries was more glamorous than realistic, at least it was wider than the vision of Ireland as seen from the mainland. Except in political or ecclesiastical circles, most Irish people in Europe found it difficult to assert their national identity, much less expect their hosts to have some idea of the island's political and cultural history.

The bond of nationalism, which was used to restore self-respect and confidence to the deprived Irish, particularly from the second half of the nineteenth century, also coloured the attitudes of Irish people in the second half of the twentieth. On one hand, much of the inspiration had originally come from the republicanism of eighteenth-century France, but the anti-Catholicism of most European radicals alienated a population which depended on its priests for leadership and help. Even when the Catholic Hierarchy condemned the physical force movements against British control of the island in the twentieth-century only a few of the leaders left the Catholic Church.

Irish nationalism developed along its own lines – perhaps the only political combination to which it was opposed in principle was the union with Great Britain. By the end of the Second World War this issue had been solved, except for the Six Counties already mentioned. There were no links with any continental nationalist movements (with the possible exception of the Bretons). Neither were there strong feelings of attachment or antagonism to any country or to any party, other than against imperial 'atheistic Communism'. Any proposal for European unity would therefore fall on virgin soil. It would not have the historical pull such ideas exercised on the 'mainland', neither would it appear as a particular threat. Its appeal, where it was acknowledged, was as a means of getting out of the straight-jacket of British-Irish preoccupations and a relationship which, after three hundred years, had become stifling.

An examination of the similarities between Ireland and the Western part of Europe during this period reveals three common factors: one, the problems raised by the immediate economic crisis; two, the shake-up of the traditional political parties; and three, relationships with the United States of America and the USSR.

Heretofore every serious problem had been met with a solution or solutions couched in Irish or Anglo-Irish terms.

Now, the problems were common to others and the answers had to be sought outside the British Isles. The proposals of General George Marshall, made in response to the post-war situation, in June 1947 for a *joint* programme for economic recovery envisaged a common reconstruction effort which would make it possible to dispense with US aid by 1953. On the political side, the end of the war saw the re-emergence on the mainland of new political parties and a re-alignment of the Left. The post-war relationships of the two major world powers and the shifting alliances in the middle also impinged on Ireland. To explain how these three factors operated requires some account of the 'run-up' to the period under review.

The Irish economy

Ireland's fuel supplies, already poor, sank to dangerously low levels in 1947, the summer of 1946 had been one of the wettest on record and as soon as goods appeared in the shops their prices rose alarmingly. Pay lagged behind and the frustration built up during the years of scarcity and restraint began to show itself in strikes, discontent with the traditional political parties and renewed IRA activity in Ireland itself.

All the Irish political parties felt the divisive effects of peacetime economic hardship. Fianna Fáil was showing signs of fatigue. It had won a General Election in May 1944, the sixth in succession, so it was naturally held directly responsible by its critics for most of the ills which beset the country. Fine Gael, the next largest party, had dropped from 44 seats at the General Election of 1938 to 31 in the Election of 1944 and put up only one candidate in the five bye-elections fought in 1945. The Labour Party, which had hoped to take the place of Fine Gael and become the main challenger to Fianna Fáil, was torn apart by the repercussions of the dispute which broke out in 1943–4 between the Irish Transport and General Workers' Union, under William O'Brien, and some of the other unions, notably the Workers' Union of Ireland, led by James Larkin (see Chapter 9). The ITGWU disaffiliated itself from the

Labour Party in 1944 and five Labour deputies who were members resigned from the Party and sat as 'National Labour' for six years, until the breach was finally healed.

The farmers' party, Clann na Talmhan, lost its deputy leader, Patrick Cogan, in 1947 and he formed a National Agricultural Party, which eventually disappeared (see Chapter 8). The Communist Party of Ireland, which never succeeded in winning a seat and had virtually disappeared from view, revived as the Irish Workers' League in 1948, and the IRA began to reorganise with Sinn Féin, the small, ultra-Republican party which claimed to be the direct descendant of the original party from which both Fianna Fáil and Fine Gael had sprung.[5]

It was fortunate that some of the steam was taken out of the situation by the formation of a new political party founded on a combination of die-hard Republicanism, social radicalism and frustrated idealism under the leadership of Seán MacBride. This party, called Clann na Poblachta, came into prominence in 1946, bringing together some idealistic figures who were new to the Irish political scene. Foremost among them were Dr Noel Browne, a lonely radical whose chequered career was to become unique in Ireland, Noel Hartnett, a barrister and broadcaster, and Jack McQuillan, who remained with Dr Noel Browne after the break-up of Clann na Poblachta in the fifties. The election of Seán MacBride in a bye-election in 1947 was a prelude to the defeat of the Fianna Fáil government in the General Election of the following year – the arrival of a new party undoubtedly helped to defuse a difficult situation throughout the country. The post-war disenchantment could have had serious repercussions had there not been a change of government and, at the same time, an opportunity to get some outside help through the Organisation for European Economic Co-operation and the European recovery programme. The attitude of the United States had not been particularly sympathetic to Irish neutrality during the war. This is understandable, since the U.S. herself had not been involved at the very beginning and, once in, naturally expected the Europeans to take their share of the brunt of the fighting.

Ryle Dwyer, an American and not a particular admirer of Mr. de Valera, makes two comments which are pertinent to the 'European' situation of Ireland.

> By the outbreak of the Second World War de Valera's international prestige was at its zenith. Ironically, the neutrality he subsequently pursued, which most Irish people – including many of his most ardent critics – considered his finest accomplishment, greatly damaged his international reputation. By the end of the war he was discredited in the eyes of many people throughout the world as a Nazi sympathiser. What made the irony even greater was the fact that he had actually pursued a neutrality which was benevolently disposed towards the Allies.[6]

However, a great impact was now felt as a result of American generosity to Europe as a whole and the encouragement given to European countries to organise and develop their recovery together. There is no sign in the 'Marshall Plan' of a policy of 'divide and rule', nor any strings, other than an anti-Communist bias, natural in the circumstances and irrelevant to Irish conditions where the Communist Party enjoyed little or no support. Two lessons, however, were painfully learned as a result of U.S. policies: firstly, that the 'Irish vote' in America was not strong enough to offset action hostile to Ireland itself if the interests of the United States seemed to require it; and, secondly, that Ireland was considered as part of Europe in the context of the recovery programme and would have to make her case in such a framework. Both were to edge Ireland closer to Europe.

Immediately after the war there was a tentative effort to rejoin the society of nations. De Valera mounted a strong, though ill-timed anti-Partition campaign in Britain, the US and throughout the English-speaking world in which he tried to 'internationalise' the issue. Seán MacBride seized on the opportunity afforded by membership of the OEEC and the Council of Europe to establish links outside the English-speaking and Irish ethnic world.

A complicating factor, but one which was to influence Irish attitudes to international organisations as a whole, was the USSR's veto on Irish entry to the United Nations. The 'bloc' embargo on a group of nations, to be lifted only in return for the entry of another group, made it quite clear to those who bothered to follow such events that small countries were regarded largely as voting fodder by the 'Big Powers'. When Ireland was eventually admitted in 1956 there was tremendous local media coverage of the contributions of her Ministers and Permanent Representatives. But no ordinary member of the Oireachtas ever managed to get to the United Nations and no resolution of that august body was likely to affect the school curriculum, the ability to trade and travel and the many aspects of ordinary life which were dealt with, directly or indirectly, by the Council of Europe and the OEEC.

The psychological effects of neutrality on Ireland during the Second World War have been colourfully described by Professor F. S. L. Lyons.

> It was as if an entire people had been condemned to live in Plato's cave, with their backs to the fire of life and deriving their only knowledge of what went on outside from the flickering shadows thrown on the wall before their eyes by the men and women who passed to and fro behind them. When after six years they emerged, dazzled, from the cave into the light of day, it was to a new and vastly different world.[7]

1948 – 51

1948 – The Congress of The Hague

The proliferation of organisations and the heavy post-war schedule of meetings, plans and policy launchings which led to a decision to co-ordinate into a single, broadly based movement favouring a united Europe, had no apparent relevance to the Irish scene. Paris had been a centre for all kinds of pro-European enthusiasts since Aristide Briand launched his proposals for a European Federation to a largely uninterested League of Nations in 1929. London had become the focal point for the more widely spread efforts of the various governments in exile to build a structure and agree on a plan of co-operation which would survive the stresses of peace and a return to normality in their home countries. After the war both London and Paris became hosts to many pro-European organisations. 'The European Union of Federalists', 'The European League for Economic Co-operation', 'The United Europe Movement', 'The Movement for a Socialist United States of Europe', 'The European Union of Christian Democrats (Nouvelles Équipes Internationales)' and 'The European Parliamentary Union' launched by the resurrected Pan-European Movement of Count Coudenhove-Kalergi were merely the more obvious and important bodies but were attended by a swarm of satellites. There were branches in most other countries and the leaders had personal contacts throughout the whole of Europe but Ireland, unlike Switzerland, found itself very much outside the scope of this activity.

European activists largely ignored Ireland. It had not been in the war. It was relatively poor. It did not pose a particular threat and therefore did not require to be mollified or challenged. Other European nations had suffered such economic and political upheavals in pre-war years that it was difficult to find time to sympathise with the trials of a young state or with its politicians, the products of an indigenous independence movement, who had spent most of the twenties and thirties trying to cope with the after-effects of civil war and the struggle for economic freedom. The League of Nations, in which Éamon de Valera had made his mark, was discredited and largely forgotten. The major Irish political parties had arisen out of a civil war (or, in the case of Clann na Poblachta, a reaction to the stagnation produced by this division) and were not members of any international political movement. Furthermore, with one exception, the younger generation of Irish politicians was unknown to its European counterparts. The exception was Seán MacBride, the Minister for External Affairs in the newly-formed first Inter-party government. MacBride had family connections abroad through both his father and mother. He spoke fluent French, and his English had such Gallic undertones that he could never be mistaken for British in even the most somnolent international assembly. As a lawyer, he had been involved in constitutional and international issues and as one of the founders of Clann na Poblachta he had formulated a new foreign policy for the party, designed to reflect a radical, positive approach to external relations. Temperament and force of circumstances made him an 'Irish European' in the context of his contemporaries.

The serious economic difficulties of the immediate post-war years had effects on international co-operation which even the enthusiasm of the new Minister for External Affairs could not overcome. Money was too scarce to provide funds for travel abroad. Even affiliation fees to international associations presented a heavy burden to Irish groups which were small in numbers and short of cash. State funds were jealously watched and little sympathy would have been given to projects to finance anything other than what was obviously of immediate benefit to industry, the unemployed, agriculture or those in need of social assistance.

It is therefore worthy of note that there was an Irish delegation at the Congress of The Hague, in May 1948, that that delegation represented two of the political parties and that the Congress was followed with considerable interest in Irish political circles. The invitation to Ireland, and the strenuous efforts to ensure that the invitation was taken up, was undoubtedly due to Joseph Retinger, the *eminence grise* of the European Movement. The archives of the College of Europe in Bruges hold the correspondence which shows his indefatigable interest in every European country, East and West, from Iceland to Turkey. Retinger was anxious to create an umbrella under which the various factions and the many nationalities would progress towards unity, rather than spend valuable time refuting each other's policies. The Congress of Europe (at The Hague), when it opened on 7 May 1948, brought together some eight hundred Europeans from twenty countries, including twenty former and future prime ministers, fifty ministers, at least two hundred and fifty members of parliament, writers like Bertrand Russell, Salvador de Madriaga, Etienne Gilson and Charles Morgan, leading lawyers, economists and academics, many trade unionists, a few industrialists and the 'leaders of all the movements for a united, federated or confederated Europe'.[1]

The Irish delegation to the Congress of Europe consisted of Senator James Douglas, Professor Michael Tierney, President of University College, Dublin and Senator Eleanor Butler of the Labour Party. Archdeacon Gordon Hannon and Frederick Thompson, both of Northern Ireland were also invited, according to telegrams in the archives in Bruges, but it was subsequently decided, probably by the organisers, that they should not be in the 'Irish' delegation.

Professor Michael Tierney had been a Senator and might therefore be classed a 'political' academic, but as it happened, his colleagues took a more active interest in the proceedings and retained their interest to a greater extent on their return. There were attempts, both before and after the Congress, to interest de Valera, then Leader of the Opposition, but he showed a notable lack of enthusiasm and this obviously affected the attitude of the Fianna Fáil party. Although the proceedings of the Congress were extensively reported in the Irish papers there is no mention of the Irish delegation nor of any contribution they may have made. They did, however, report back to Seán MacBride, as Minister for External Affairs, on their return and Lady Wicklow believes that she, as Senator Butler, was influential in persuading William Norton, the leader of the Irish Labour Party, to take an active part in the early days of the formation of the Council of Europe and to deliver a strong 'pro-European' speech to the Assembly.

After the Congress, the International Committee of United European Movements which had been formed to organise it, became *'The European Movement'* with Retinger as Secretary General and Duncan Sandys as President. The programmes outlined by the special committees set up during the Congress were publicised and led, remarkably quickly, to proposals for a Council of Europe. Even more extraordinarily the Council came into being only nine months later. The various resolutions passed at The Hague were presented to national governments by influential advocates and were largely adopted. Perhaps one of the most important resolutions (passed by the Economic Committee) was that setting out the guide-lines for a large common market, based on the merging of French and German interests. Other ideas were formulated by the Cultural and Educational Committee which led to the establishment of the Centre Europeènne de la Culture and, at a further remove, to the encouragement on the part of many departments of education, of moves to foster better understanding between young Europeans of different nationalities.

Back in Ireland, Senator Douglas found the position difficult, though he promised Retinger that he would look out 'for a suitable opportunity of initiating a discussion in the Senate'.[2] Retinger wrote to Most Rev. Dr John Charles McQuaid, the Catholic Archbishop of Dublin, whom he had already met in Dublin, mentioning the involvement of

Spaak, Churchill, de Gasperri, Cardinal Griffin and Sir Stafford Cripps, and asking the Archbishop to become the President of an Irish National Council of the European Movement.[3] Nothing further is heard of this, although Retinger kept up his contacts with Dr McQuaid and wrote to him and visited him several times in later years.

The first indication to people at home of the attitudes of Irish politicians came in the debate on foreign affairs following the formation of the Inter-Party government. Seán MacBride, as the new Minister for External Affairs, made a statement about developments in Europe which were likely to impinge on Ireland in the future. Éamon de Valera, as leader of the Opposition and spokesman on foreign affairs, replied on an equally statesmanlike level and there was a relevant speech by Sir John Esmonde (Fine Gael). But after that extraneous matters were raised and the standard of debate by subsequent speakers rapidly deteriorated to personal abuse.[4]

The Minister's reference to a United States of Europe was challenged by Major Vivion de Valera (Fianna Fáil) and MacBride returned to the subject in his reply.

> I referred to it (United States of Europe) not to suggest that it was a practical possibility at the moment, but to convey to the House that it was one of the plans that are being discussed in Europe at present, not by Governments but by Parliaments in Europe independently of Governments. We here should try to keep abreast of political developments in the international sphere, we should know what things are being discussed by them and we should think out our attitude in advance.[5]

An organisation with more immediate appeal for Irish politicians than a 'United States of Europe' at this time was the Organisation for European Economic Co-operation, set up in 1947 and inspired by a US desire to see a co-ordinated effort at post-war reconstruction in Europe. The idea was actively embraced by Seán Lemass who was then Minister for Industry and Commerce, and Seán MacBride, as Minister for External Affairs, played an even

B

more active role in the Organisation after the change of government.

The OEEC itself underwent three different phases in the period covered by this study. The first was from 1948-51 when the main job was the distribution of US aid, which itself was conditional on trade and payments liberalisation and inter-European co-operation. The second phase was from 1952-56, when the process of removing obstacles to intraregional commerce continued, even though US aid had ceased. From 1956 the issues of economic co-operation and integration became enmeshed with the political issues of 'the Six' versus 'the Seven' and fundamental changes in national policies interrupted the smooth progress of the Organisation's work.

During the first phase the typical OEEC procedure for gaining multinational support worked through 'confrontation, collection of detailed information, mediation in closed sessions and the working out of specific solutions to crises by autonomous bodies of national experts.'[6]

Why should such a straightforward, if cumbrous, formula work? Because the national policies of most of the member countries at the time were in favour of liberalisation and because the OEEC procedure of 'splitting the difference' resulted in successful compromises, each of which advanced the level of co-operation to a higher level.

It is a paradox that it is easier in many ways to trace the attitudes of sections of Irish public opinion to European integration and their evolution during the late forties and fifties than to present a comprehensive study of official government policy on the same issue over the same period. If a Minister makes a speech linking Ireland to European affairs and is not contradicted by any of his colleagues, does that mean they support his view or regard it as a relatively harmless eccentricity to which he is entitled? Or could it be that the Cabinet was constantly and carefully monitoring events on the mainland and decided to preserve a massive silence in order to keep open for the future as many diplomatic options as possible?

Speeches by the Taoiseach and Minister for External Affairs to the Houses of the Oireachtas are the obvious sources for inklings on foreign policy. Yet, on the whole, the Dáil Reports show little more than unexceptional statements in favour of peace, good-will and international co-operation and, on occasion, spirited defence of the staff of External Affairs, particularly when they were under attack for over-activity, under-action, or merely as unnecessary trappings of luxury.

The Taoiseach of the Inter-Party Government which gained power in 1948, John A. Costello, was a member of Fine Gael and the Minister for External Affairs was Seán MacBride, one of the founders of Clann na Poblachta. Both were barristers but there the resemblance ended. Costello was a long-time member of Fine Gael but he was not the party leader and his views on external relations were not an electoral issue before he came to office. MacBride, on the other hand, had founded his party on a new version of radical republicanism and a fairly sweeping change of both style and policy was expected of him. Costello had been a prominent spokesman of foreign affairs for Fine Gael since his entry into the Dáil in 1933 and had criticised public apathy about the formulation and direction of foreign policy in the debate on the League of Nations estimate in 1936.[7] The position was further complicated by the fact that Fine Gael and Clann na Poblachta had taken different positions on whether or not Ireland should secede from the British Commonwealth in the General Election campaign of 1948 which returned them to power. The government's subsequent decision to leave the Commonwealth cleared away the 'Commonwealth' as an alternative to an association with 'Europe' when the latter became an option.

The main preoccupations in Ireland in the autumn of 1948, however, were the difficulties of trying to improve incomes, coping with unemployment and fostering industry and agriculture. Indeed, agriculture dominated the Irish economy to a great extent in the immediate post-war era but its exports were almost totally dependent on the British market and discussions centred, not on opportunities in Europe, which were non-existent, but on the prices that could be wrung from London. Grave concern was even being expressed about the effects of the Anglo-Irish Trade agreement, described by industry as 'inequitable, one-sided, and greatly to the disadvantage of industrial continuance and development in Ireland'.[8]

1949 – The Council of Europe

The removal of Ireland in 1949 from Commonwealth deliberations imperceptibly strengthened the pull towards Europe. Since no place was available in the United Nations and a decision had been made not to seek membership of NATO,[9] it was fortunate that the invitation to take part in the Council of Europe came that year. There was no further excuse for pretending that Irish feelings about Suez, the Middle East, British foreign policy in Africa or the revolution in China received any serious consideration outside the country.

The Council of Europe was considered therefore to be very important for Ireland and the government of the day, particularly the Taoiseach, John A. Costello, and the Minister for External Affairs, Seán MacBride, were well aware of the various draft proposals for the Council's constitution. MacBride took the opportunity provided by a Motion to approve the Statute of the Council of Europe to make a major speech in the Dáil in which he expressed his strong disapproval of the compromise formula which had finally been agreed, and gave the deputies a historical picture of the background of European Union. He dwelt on the question of economic co-operation under the umbrella of the OEEC. He then declared what he thought was wrong with the Statute under discussion.

> To a large extent the statute which is presented to the House is designed to shackle the members of the Assembly but I feel that, with the passage of time, the members of the Assembly themselves will take things into their own hands. . . . That may be bad for the Foreign Ministers concerned, but it may be quite good for the development of the idea of European Federation.[10]

It seems unlikely that, with the exception of Robert Schuman in France, many of MacBride's ministerial colleagues spoke in similar terms. In the other member countries it was more likely to be the parliamentarians who protested at the clipping of the Assembly's wings.

Although the Irish government was obviously informed of developments, there was apparently only one Irish delegate at the Paris meeting to draft the Statute and draw up the agenda for the Consultative Assembly in Strasbourg in 1949. That was Senator Eleanor Butler, who had attended the Congress of The Hague the previous year, but who did not consider herself a legal, constitutional or political expert. She is reported as being more than somewhat apprehensive:

> When I got to Paris the night before and found I was the only one, I was panic-stricken. I remember the Irish Ambassador telling me to stick to the Danish Foreign Minister and together we got our points on the agenda.[11]

The lack of participation in the drafting stages may explain the preferences of the long-established Irish political parties for the traditional, inter-governmental organisation such as OEEC. The Assembly of the Council of Europe was a new concept in Irish politics and subsequent attendance and involvement in the Assembly, when it came into being, is all the more remarkable because most of the Irish politicians had missed the prologue.

Other participating countries were involved at government or at least parliamentary and political levels and used the negotiations to get some of their own ideas incorporated into the final design.

How near the 'miss' was in some respects can be gauged from the evidence in the College of Europe archives in Bruges. A letter, dated 4 November 1949, from Senator James Douglas to M. G. Rebattet (Paris Secretary of the European Movement which had both a Paris and London office at this time), says that

> The Irish Parliamentary Group met on November 2nd and appointed the following officers. Senator J. C.

> Douglas, Chairman, Deputy M. Dockrell, Hon. Treasurer, Senator J. Crosbie, Hon. Sec. and Mr. M. Christie, Clerk of the Senate. At present the group consists of members of both Houses of Parliament and a letter is being sent out to all Senators and Deputies which may result in a somewhat increased membership.

The letter does not reveal, however, that *all* the parliamentarians mentioned were members of the Fine Gael Party.

There were occasions over the years when the Irish parliamentarians became officially or accidentally involved in meetings of the International Parliamentary Group of the European Movement or even of the somewhat shadowy Pan-Europa Union of Count Coudenhove-Kalergi. But they never showed a sustained interest in setting up a 'professional' group in Ireland. It may be that lack of knowledge of languages other than Irish and English, allied to the lack of personal enthusiasm of the leaders of the three largest political parties at the time, plus lack of money, dulled the attraction of European meetings for the great majority of Irish politicians.

Whatever the support for European co-operation on the economic plane, there is little doubt that the Partition question affected the role played by Irish delegates in the early days of the Council of Europe. Both de Valera and MacBride wanted to raise the matter internationally, but the problem, however largely it loomed on the Irish horizon was not considered a sufficient reason for offending Britain by German, French and Italian leaders, faced as they were by troubles such as the Saar and Trieste and the threat of Russian encroachments. However, in spite of what they may have considered a disappointing response to the partition issue, the Irish sent a very strong delegation to the first sessions of the Assembly of the Council of Europe in Strasbourg.[12]

Once arrived in Strasbourg, the Irish representatives set to work. Churchill is reported as supporting a resolution sponsored by de Valera, Norton and a representative from Norway to curb the power of the Council of Ministers and MacBride expressed himself pleased with this move.[13] It did not, however, succeed. On another issue the front page of *The Irish Press* of 7 September 1949 had banner headlines: DE VALERA FIGHTS FOR CULTURAL REPORT AMENDMENT – UNITY OF EUROPE TALKS PLANNED FOR ROME. A report from Strasbourg follows, incorporating the warm debate on the Report of the Cultural Committee. Senator Finan (FF) and Seán MacEntee (FF) had objected to the use of the phrase, 'to satisfy the vital needs of the workers'. Apparently 'workers' was felt to refer merely to organised labour, and the British Conservatives and Fianna Fáil argued that the term was too restrictive and that all citizens, including parliamentarians, were entitled to help in the development of their cultural life. In his speech on the issue de Valera stated 'To me European Unity is not an end in itself, it is a means to an end' and the end he envisaged was the cultural, social and economic progress, in a gradual way, of all the peoples of Europe. For the political scientist supporter of the traditional functionalist approach the attraction of enlightened self-interest was inevitable. 'Beneath the different national costumes he hears the beat of the heart of economic man'[14] wrote one such. But de Valera's heart was, on the evidence of his own actions and policies, far from being that of simple 'economic man'. Nor would he have been likely to agree about the disruptive effects of nationalism.

Ten nations were represented at the early sessions of the Consultative Assembly of the Council of Europe. The opening address by M. Edouard Herriot set the historical background (recalling Aristide Briand's dreams of the twenties), and then gave warm tribute to Winston Churchill, 'for in many moments of deep tragedy he bore upon his shoulders the whole weight of the world crying out for help. From his mind sprang the movement which has brought us together here'[15] and finally raised the problem of the absent German nation. 'It is therefore for Germany herself to reply to a question which for us, raises a moral, even more than a political problem.'

From their interventions it is apparent that the Irish politicians misjudged the depth of the feeling of gratitude to Churchill on the part of those of other nationalities and political complexion, even those who may have personally disliked or been wary of him. This post-war euphoria stretched from Norway to France and made Irish antagonism to Britain's tenure of Northern Ireland quite a dissonant note. Secondly, while well aware intellectually of the problem of the reconciliation of the infant democracy of the Federal Republic of Germany with her former enemies and the dilemma of the East German Democratic Republic, firmly under Communist control, the Irish delegates do not seem to have appreciated how such a situation made the partition of Ireland appear of minor significance.

The most sweeping condemnation of the contribution of the Irish politicians is that of Dr Conor Cruise O'Brien:

> Our Parliamentary delegates to the Council of Europe seemed to devote their time to making speeches about partition; speeches which were designed to be read at home, but which unfortunately had to be listened to abroad.[16]

However much the subject may have embarrassed Dr Cruise O'Brien, there is no evidence to suggest that William Norton, Éamon de Valera, Seán MacEntee and their colleagues did not hope to sway their continental audience to put some pressure on Britain to change a situation which they considered to be unjust and a source of potential trouble between Ireland and Britain in the future. Nor was it the only matter on which the Irish delegation spoke. William Norton, the Tánaiste and Leader of the Labour Party, took the initiative on the first day and helped to force an election of the four Vice-Presidents after the non-contested elevation of Paul Henri Spaak to the Presidency. He also intervened about the need to appoint a Secretary General and Deputy Secretary General who would be responsible to the Assembly and not to the Council of Ministers as was envisaged in the Statutes. 'This Assembly is in the nature of being a Parliament of Europe; one day it may be the Parliament of Europe.'[17] He was supported by Lord Boothby, among others, and, though overruled on the point, was appointed to the Credentials Committee. There was considerable confusion about rules, procedure and points of order during the first session, which was hardly surprising considering the different parliamentary traditions of the members. The 'lost' feeling of many of the delegates was expressed by Seán MacEntee when he commented: 'It has been somewhat difficult for those of us who have not attended a conference of this sort before to know exactly what facilities we have at our disposal.' This concern was echoed by delegates from other countries.

When it came to the general debate of political development (the 5th Sitting on 15 August 1949), Norton did indeed raise the subject of the partition of Ireland, making it clear that one of the reasons he did so was to reach an international audience, explaining that his country was denied access to the United Nations because of the Soviet veto, though he indicated that he was not too worried about the deprivation of membership of 'that monster of peace'. When de Valera's turn came he began by outlining the division between the two main trends within the Assembly, that of rapid federalist and gradualist approaches.

He gave credit to each side and continued:

> In both cases I believe that the chief urge is of a practical character and that the difference depends on the fact that the people of the mainland have had this question of the political unity of Europe, and all that it involves, discussed more widely in public than have the peoples in the Island of Britain or our own people in Ireland.

He went on to support Norton's stand on the partition of Ireland. Returning to the immediate problem of the Assembly, however, de Valera suggested immediate practical co-operation on economic matters and a further study of the implication of political unity. He expressed his fears about the difficulties which he saw as inevitable.

> It is because I am acutely conscious of these difficulties that I am in favour of a more gradual approach. In that I find myself in agreement to a large extent with the conservative attitude which has been indicated here and,

I might say, with the British attitude as I have been able to understand it.

When he returned to power, de Valera could not, even if he had so desired, play an active role in the Council of Europe, but it is apparent that he never saw it as the nucleus of a European Parliament or anything more than an instrument of co-operation. In two interviews, one in 1952 and another in 1954, he gave the kernel of his attitude to the Council of Europe. Speaking to Associated Press, when asked what was the difference between Ireland's active participation in the Council of Europe and her refusal to join NATO, Mr de Valera replied:

> Membership of the Council of Europe imposes on us no obligation which is inconsistent with our national rights. Membership of NATO, on the other hand, implies acceptance by each member of the territorial integrity of each of the several States comprising it.[18]

A long interview, given in 1954, explains in retrospect the thinking of the Fianna Fáil leader at the time of the creation of the Council of Europe. In this interview de Valera dealt specifically with the prospect of European Federation. He said that,

> . . . in his younger days, over thirty years ago, he had been an ardent supporter of the idea of a United States of Europe, but that, in recent years, he had become more aware of the magnitude of the difficulties involved. If, for example, Ireland entered into such a Federation her representation in the proposed legislature would probably be so small as to be ineffective, and matters vital to the Irish people could be easily ignored. Ireland's representation in the Council of Europe was now only 4 out of a total of 132.
>
> The idea of a complete political Federation of Europe was most attractive, but when one got down to the details it was not easy to find a workable scheme. . . . The larger states, such as France, Germany, Italy, might in the existing circumstances be willing to join such a Federation, each being confident that they were suffi-

ciently powerful to ensure that matters vital to them would not be overlooked. But it was not so with the smaller States. They would of course have gained the security of the collective strength, but they would have lost the power to choose at will policies required to meet their individual political and economic exigencies. To this extent they would have lost their independence. Was the price too high? That was the critical question in regard to a close federal political union for Europe, such as that of the existing United States of America.

Close co-operation for specific purposes, such as the Schuman plan – the 'European Coal and Steel Community' – was quite a different matter, and he believed, in present circumstances, that that was the most fruitful line to pursue.[19]

The constituency of County Clare, which returned de Valera to Dáil Éireann with loyal fervour at each election, enjoyed, over the years, a roughly similar proportion of seats but it could hardly be argued that the interests of its electors had been ignored or their representative considered ineffective. De Valera's view must therefore have been coloured by his impressions in the Council of Europe, firstly, that there was not as much common interest as existed between the different parts of Ireland and secondly, that the Irish delegates had not been able to make a major impact on the views of their European colleagues.

The reports on the Second Session of the Council of Europe confirm a certain lack of empathy between Irish delegates and the rest. When MacEntee rose to speak on the subject of Human Rights, the President (M. Spaak) had to intervene to protest, 'We must not allow every Debate to become the object of a dispute between the Representatives of Ireland and Great Britain. . . . I beg you to keep to the matter in hand,'[20] and when, the following year, the Assembly came to debate Winston Churchill's proposal for a European Army, the chair had to intervene to ask the Irish delegates (Norton, de Valera and MacEntee) to respect the rights of others to have the floor, begging, 'do not let us have a repetition of last year!'. The combination of

Churchill, army and territorial rights was too much for the Irish, however, and the Assembly did have 'a repetition' of the acrimony.

There were long debates on economic and even monetary union and Frank Aiken, then in Opposition, spoke on this issue rather than on partition at the first meeting of the Consultative Assembly he attended in 1949. 'The proposal of a customs union, as I see it,' said Aiken, 'means in practice the most wholesale and the most rapid uprooting and re-deployment of working populations and capital equipment ever effected, with, as far as I know, but one exception.' He went on to deplore its short-term and long-term possible social and economic consequences and to suggest, instead, the adoption of proposals he had made in 1933 to the London Economic Conference, updated, to have an agreed international monetary unit. This line, to which Aiken returned later and which was supported by de Valera, did not find much favour in the Assembly.

1950 – The Year of Coal and Steel

It had become apparent in 1949 that Britain was not prepared to commit herself fully to any real economic and political integration of Europe, so the decision to develop a European Coal and Steel Community was taken by Belgium, France, Luxembourg, Italy, the Netherlands and West Germany. Because Britain was not involved and neither coal nor steel played any major role in the Irish economy (other than as imports) there was almost no public discussion on the implications for Ireland of the new body.

1950 was, however, an eventful year in the life of the Council of Europe. Iceland, the Saar and the Federal Republic of Germany took their places in the assembly and M. Spaak, when proposed for the Presidency, was vehemently opposed by a delegate from the Netherlands and Seán MacEntee. This was obviously because of the Belgian constitutional crisis earlier in the year in which M. Spaak had played a role disapproved of by his opponents. He was nonetheless elected and the highlights of the first session were the contributions of Robert Schuman and of Seán MacBride, who had the difficult task of defending, or at least explaining, the Council of Ministers to an irate Assembly.[21]

The Council of Europe, and the OEEC, gradually became more familiar names in Ireland and the fact that Seán MacBride became a Vice-President of OEEC in February 1950 added to the 'local interest'. The business community was beginning to take an active interest in European tariff and trade barriers and *The Farmers' Journal* of that year reflects the concern of the agricultural community in the economic progress of Europe. On June 3 1950 the paper speculated,

> The countries of Europe need Irish food and Ireland needs free access to their markets. If the proposed new arrangement should be achieved then it might well mean the end of partition and the entry of Ireland fully into a Europe secure in its strength and rid of most of the barriers which to-day prevent free movement and trade among nations.

The proposed new arrangement was the political and economic strengthening of NATO and its extension into the non-military field.

During its August meeting the Consultative Assembly of the Council of Europe considered the 'Schuman Plan' and recommended the creation of a single, integrated European army. (The voting was 89 in favour, 5 against – the five being 1 British Labour, plus 4 Irish, with 27 abstentions.) Seán MacBride would have favoured the European Defense Community (EDC), but he had become President of the Council of Foreign Ministers and his opinions were not shared by the Irish delegation, even those belonging to parties which supported him in government. Perhaps Irish representatives were simply more open in their voting than those parliamentarians who subsequently dragged their feet until they were 'forced' to yield to the pressure of their more intransigent colleagues and abandon the whole idea. Nevertheless, it is clear that their

'European' spirit was not strong enough to enable them to swallow the concept of Irish soldiers serving with, under and over British soldiers – even though such a force would be well diluted with French, Italians, Germans and the rest.

In July 1950, when introducing the estimates for the Department of External Affairs, Seán MacBride began with Europe, giving a fairly long summary of developments in the Council of Europe and then dealing with events farther afield.[22] There followed an interesting contribution from Mr. de Valera which throws some light on the divergence on Europe between Fianna Fáil and the government, or perhaps just between de Valera and MacBride. 'At Strasbourg' said Mr. de Valera,

> I felt that the Government had the same kind of approach to the Council and its work as some of the continental representatives. They thought they had a Parliament of Europe and that they could immediately divide themselves up into political Parties with the Committee of Ministers as a kind of Cabinet of Europe. I felt that was a line upon which we could not proceed, certainly for a very long time to come. . . . Some recent statements I have seen from the Government side seem to indicate that I was wrong then in thinking that the Government was proceeding on that particular line.[23]

The EDC caused no serious debate in Ireland and by November European affairs were back in the headlines along different lines. The Mansholt plan for a single European market for farming products caused considerable interest, not only in the farming press but also among Irish economists and business interests.

The real discussion at this time, however, centred on the proposals to ratify the Convention on Human Rights proposed by the Consultative Assembly of the Council of Europe and designed to give binding force to its Articles in all the member states. There was a genuine concern in Ireland for human rights, but there was also a tactical feeling that such a Convention could be used to press for changes in the conditions of the Catholic minority in Northern Ireland.

The Convention for the Protection of Human Rights and Fundamental Freedoms, to give its full and proper title, was signed by Ireland on 4th February 1950, deposited on 25th February 1953 and came into force on 3rd September 1953. As an issue it gained public attention with the Lawless Case. Gerard Lawless was detained on 13 July 1957 under Section 4 of Offences against the State (Amendment) Act 1940. He claimed that such detention, without having been brought before a judge for trial, was in conflict with the Irish government's obligations under Sections 5, 6 and 7 of the European Convention of Human Rights. It was also claimed that a letter of 20 July 1957 from the Irish government to the Secretary General of the Council of Europe did not constitute sufficient notice of derogation for the purposes of Article 15, par. 3 of the Convention. The Court eventually found in favour of the Irish government on all counts. The case only finished before the European Court of Human Rights in 1960 and naturally received publicity at each stage of the legal process.

This aspect of European integration raised issues of legal sovereignty which were more basic than many of the proposals for economic integration at which the Irish delegates had taken such fright, but was hardly criticised at all during the period. There was an unspoken impression that it would be some other country, probably the United Kingdom, which would be taken before the Court.

1951 – Change of Government

The drive towards European integration accelerated in 1951. The Treaty of the European Coal and Steel Community was formally signed in April, the Federal Republic of Germany became a full member of the Council of Europe in May, the OEEC started a European campaign for increasing agricultural production and adopted a Code for the Liberalisation of Trade and, finally, in December the Council of Europe was recommending the creation of a 'European Authority for Agriculture', the formation of a 'Low Tariff Club' and looking for a conference on European Air Transport (to sort out the anomalies and restrictions which were bedevilling the attempts to increase traffic in people and goods).

1951 started badly for the Inter-Party government. A transport strike dragged on from December, the bank officials threatened strike action (which they took), the balance of payments deficit was running higher than ever before and efforts to reduce it put an increasing strain on the government itself and on its relations with the population at large. There were also rumblings from the medical profession and the Catholic Hierarchy that a proposed new health scheme to provide free medical care for all mothers and all children up to the age of sixteen was unacceptable – for different reasons – to both bodies.

On 7 March 1951 all the Irish papers carried a release from the Government Information Bureau giving details of the Mother and Child Scheme. It soon became obvious that the other members of the Cabinet, in particular those belonging to Fine Gael, were not prepared to back Dr Browne; indeed some of them apparently themselves disapproved of the scheme. On 12 April 1951 the Taoiseach, John A. Costello, accepted the resignation of Dr Browne and took over the Ministry of Health himself. Dr Browne also resigned from Clann na Poblachta and there was no surprise at all when the Dáil was dissolved and a General Election called for 30 May. As a result of this election Clann na Poblachta were almost wiped out; the results showed: Fianna Fáil 69; Inter-Party 64; Independents 14 – an extraordinarily high number of independents for Ireland. When the time came to elect a Taoiseach, Éamon de Valera was returned 74 votes to 69, even though his party did not have an overall majority in the Dáil. Such a situation did not permit the new government to pursue adventurous policies either in foreign affairs or economic expansion and the tight-rope continued for the next three years.

The period in opposition gave Fianna Fáil the opportunity to start a gradual retreat from the policy of protectionism with which they had built up the economy at an earlier stage. On Fianna Fáil's return to power the party was much more open to suggestions that Ireland might participate in some kind of Free Trade Association. There were two main difficulties. The first was the severe economic hardship already being endured and the danger of adding dramatically to it before there was some specific aid to cushion the blow. The second was the fear of losing the British market before Irish industry and agriculture had managed to secure a firm footing in European alternatives.

In the early fifties there were constant changes in the different delegations to the Council of Europe, including those from Ireland. At the Third Ordinary Session of 1951, Gerald Boland made his maiden speech to the Assembly, objecting to proposals to amend tariffs, and commenting that the long-established industries in Ireland were situated 'in a part of the country which has been cut off by the 1920 Act of the British Parliament'. He stated that the removal of tariffs would be in the interests of the countries proposing such measures and indicated that Ireland was governed by the same principles of self-interest. 'At the same time we are very much interested indeed in the European movement; we wish it well, and anything that will not directly interfere with the progress of our own country we shall be most happy to support.'[24] Senator James Crosbie (Fine Gael) returned to the same point, in more sophisticated terms, referring to the impossibility of Ireland's entering an agreement to abolish customs or even a Low Tariff Club. (He also made a graceful passing reference to his complete agreement with his 'distinguished fellow-countryman, Mr. Harden of the British delegation, who represents another portion of Ireland'.) M. Motz (Belgium), who was the chairman of the sub-committee responsible for the report replied to these objections, among others. 'Our Irish friends spoke to-day and pointed out that their country was in a difficult position. Let me say, however, that, according to the information they have given me, it appears that potential developments in Ireland's agricultural economy are most promising'.

He went on to deal with Irish reservations about the Low Tariff Club and made it clear that Ireland was not the target of the customs union lobby.

The General Election which returned a Fianna Fáil government to power in 1951, the economic situation at home and a general feeling that 'Europe' was going a bit too fast for comfort, combined to diminish discussion on European topics for some time. The tone of the new government's policy was set by Frank Aiken's first speech as Minister for External Affairs to the Dáil when he began by acknowledging what Marshall Aid had done for the country. Seán MacBride made a 'statesmanlike' speech, to which Aiken briefly replied, but there was no indication of any positive government policy towards European integration. This pattern was repeated during the succeeding years. There were still reports from the Council of Europe in the newspapers and on radio but the impetus seems to have passed from the politicians for a time. Reports of occasional events, such as the address of William Taft to the TCD Association for International Affairs on 'European Unity' when Judge Gavan Duffy, President of the High Court, spoke on Ireland's contribution to the Council of Europe and expressed the hope that Ireland would participate in the College of Europe to be set up in Bruges to promote European studies, indicate that the initiative passed to non-political bodies.[25]

The Trough of Depression 1952 – 57

Politically and economically 1952 was a depressing year for Ireland, and it is hardly surprising that the tentative feelers which had been put out towards Europe hurriedly retreated or died. Realisation also dawned that continually raising the question of partition in Strasbourg with 'the double aim of embarrassing Britain and enlisting foreign sympathy for the Irish case' was not achieving any practical results. F. S. L. Lyons sums up the problem:

> In Strasbourg certainly, where Ireland became a founder member of the Council of Europe in 1949 and used the Assembly for some years thereafter as one of the main platforms for anti-partition speeches, the reaction among other delegates seems to have been one of boredom mingled with bewilderment.[1]

With hindsight, it is possible to argue that the fester of partition should have been taken more seriously by the British and the Europeans.

The Fianna Fáil government had come to power with the support of Independent deputies and faced a serious economic recession, a resurgence of IRA activity and a growing demand for better health and social services, without an overall majority in the Dáil. Éamon de Valera brought back most of his previous Ministers but he gave Frank Aiken the portfolio for External Affairs, an acknowledgment perhaps of the growth of Ireland's international activity, since he had previously looked after that Department himself.

In 1952 the two major debating subjects in the Council of Europe were still defence and the manner in which economic and political 'co-operation' should be effected. The European Defence Community Proposals had been signed by the Six and to some extent 'guaranteed' by the United States of America while the British Conservative government, under Anthony Eden, put forward some supplementary proposals (which were interpreted by most of the Federalists as counter-proposals) to link the EDC with the Council of Europe. The British were also critical of the decision to go ahead with the European Coal and Steel Community. The atmosphere of the Consultative Assembly was distinctly frosty. At this stage Senator Finan (Clann na Talmhan) intervened with a shrewd and frank speech which must have made a good impression. Referring to the criticisms of the Coal and Steel Community proposals and the danger that such an arrangement would represent to the British coal and steel industries, Finan felt that these fears could be allayed and declared himself in favour of the Community. He then went on to grasp the second nettle.

> I think, notwithstanding all that has been said here in regard to the Eden Plan, that my quarrel would be with the fact that, as far as I understand it, it is not a plan at all. It contains vague proposals . . . . But I do say this much: that it would be infinitely desirable that the closest possible links which can be forged should exist between the Six Powers and the Council of Europe.[2]

He regretted the inability of the other UK representatives, particularly the Conservatives, to clarify Eden's proposals. He understood them to support the autonomy of the political authority of the ECSC but that the Community should act in co-operation with the decisions and wishes of the Council of Europe. He defended Spaak for what appeared to him as a logical position: to pursue the solution which he, Spaak, believed in, in the company of those who were of like mind. This speech is in contrast to that of Gerald Boland who returned, once again, to the historical wrongs of Ireland.

In September all papers gave good coverage to the Consultative Assembly of the European Coal and Steel Community and to Paul Henri Spaak's election as its first president. (He had been succeeded as President of the Consultative Assembly of the Council of Europe by de Menthon.) In all of this there is, however, a certain air of remoteness. The Presidential Election in the United States, the formal declaration of peace between the US and Japan and the Russian purges (which were to prove Stalin's last) were all dealt with in much the same way.

1953–4

The continuing flow of emigrants undoubtedly helped to keep the Irish political situation relatively stable, albeit depressed. The pattern of emigration was, however, changing and the unskilled emigrants to Britain and the Commonwealth were now joined by a high proportion of graduates, as well as an increased number of nurses, teachers and administrators.

Because of language difficulties and the non-recognition of diplomas and professional qualifications between Ireland and the continental countries of Europe there was no appreciable emigration in that direction. There was therefore still no incentive for those who intended going abroad to look very closely at Western Europe.

Emigration and unemployment were not the only problems on the horizon in 1953. The row over Dr Noel Browne's 'Mother and Child Scheme', which had brought down the inter-party government in 1951 had left the vacuum in health legislation which Fianna Fáil was pledged to fill. In July 1952, Dr Ryan, the Minister for Health, issued a white paper outlining his intentions and in February 1953 he published the text of a health bill which proposed to deal not only with mother and child welfare but a wide range of other health issues as well.[3] The debate on health legislation showed the remarkable distrust of centralised state control which existed, not only in the ranks of the Catholic Hierarchy, in Ireland. Many extraneous issues were dragged in but this issue was crucial; almost twenty years later advocates of Ireland's entry into the European Community were careful to emphasise the strengthening of regions and peripheral areas which would follow entry into the big, diversified Community. (Whether their hopes were justified is, of course, another matter.)

There is a temptation to link the decline in the ambitions of European Federalists which took place after 1954 (when all, except the most zealous maximalists, accepted that national governments in Europe were unwilling to merge their sovereign powers) with an increased interest in federal principles in Ireland. The European federalists divided in 1956 with the split over revolutionary versus evolutionary methods and tactics.[4] The evolutionary wing of the Federal Movement, led by Professor Brugmans who was known and liked in Ireland, might have been expected to have a good deal of appeal. Federalism, of either variety, tries to combine political union between states with the exercise of authority diffused so that it operates at whatever is the most appropriate level. As far as political union was concerned, it had always been seen as a possible solution to the problem of uniting the two parts of Ireland by those who wished for such a union while rejecting force as a solution and recognised the complexity of the Northern Ireland situation. Its other aspect, the diffusion of the authority of the unitary, centralised state and the participation in the exercise of authority by local or regional units should have appealed to the anti-centralist feelings revealed in the struggle over the apparently unlikely subject of medical services.

Surprisingly Seán MacBride, in opposition, did not use the European Movement as a base from which the interest in European developments he showed as Minister for External Affairs might have had a domestic impact. He certainly maintained his personal contacts with many European statesmen and attended such meetings as were arranged in Dublin, but the need to return to his law practice, plus the attempts to rebuild Clann na Poblachta after its poor showing in the 1951 General Election absorbed most of his energies. Also, any movement seen to be inspired by Seán MacBride would have been viewed with more than the usual suspicion by other politicians and by non-political leaders. There were, however, several tentative efforts to get some sort of Irish Council of the European Movement off the ground and although there was no Irish representative at the Second Congress of The Hague in 1953, Ireland was invited, through Donal O'Sullivan, to send four delegates to the Congress of Westminster from 29 January to 1 February 1954.

The foundation of the first Irish Council of the European Movement in 1954 is covered in a later part of this study, but it should be set against the background in which defence was a key issue in the current European debate. Defence was, and is, a prickly issue in Ireland. The European Defence Community was regarded with some favour in Irish circles which followed the debate 'on the mainland'. Apart altogether from the question of Northern Ireland, the idea of 'foreign bases' in Ireland and the political and financial implications of membership of NATO were not acceptable to many Irish people but the new idea of a genuinely multi-national defence force had no particular prejudices to overcome. None of the political parties raised the issue however and the economic and political ties which the European Defence Community required were still considered out of reach, in practical terms, by the Irish. This did not stop 'Irish-European' circles from taking a high moral tone towards the British and the French, who were jointly considered the wreckers of the idea. In August 1954 *The Leader* had a censorious article entitled 'The End of E.D.C.' in which Mendes-France and the French politicians were severely reprimanded for their non-co-operative attitude towards European defence. The writer approved of the EDC and saw it as an acceptable alternative to NATO; this view was quite widespread in 'Irish-European' circles.[5]

There was no report in Irish papers of the time of the Conference of European Socialists which met in Brussels to consider the proposal to form the EDC, perhaps because there appears to have been no Irish participation. There was very little interest in European affairs in Irish labour or trade union circles at this time.

The Fianna Fáil government had been in a precarious position since it came into office in 1951 and it went once again into opposition in 1954 when the Inter-Party government returned to power. This coalition was, however, different in some important respects from its predecessor. Clann na Poblachta was not represented and Liam Cosgrave took over the post of Minister for External Affairs, formerly held by Seán MacBride. Cosgrave was elected chairman of the Council of Ministers of the Council of Europe in 1955, and this honour was widely reported in Ireland, but it was a Council of Europe which had been shorn of much of its political promise and prestige by the creation of the European Community of 'the Six' and the Council of Europe's own inability to live up to the leading role in European integration which had been the reason behind its creation. Cosgrave discharged his duties conscientiously but does not seem to have attempted any innovations, either on the European or Irish scene. With the exception of the issue on Human Rights neither the Assembly nor the Council of Ministers sparked off any major controversy during the middle fifties. Its effects on Irish attitudes to Europe were gradual and not easily classified.

Neither is it easy to assess the changes, if any, in government attitudes. In 1954 Liam Cosgrave, as Minister for External Affairs, merely presented the estimates for his Department to the Dáil, but the following year he spoke at some length, linking the question of Partition and European co-operation.

> Isolation or aggressive policies tend to divide us more and more fundamentally from the majority of our fellow-countrymen in the Six Counties. On the other hand, the more we direct our activities towards playing a part suitable to our means and geographical position in the solution of the great problems that confront Western Europe as a whole, the more it will become apparent to the people of the Six Counties also that their destiny is one with ours, just as ours is one with the peoples of Western Europe.[6]

Later in his speech Cosgrave congratulated members of the Irish delegation to the Consultative Assembly of the Council of Europe (of all parties) on their contributions there and reviewed the activities of the Council of Ministers of the Council of Europe and of the OEEC. In reply de Valera reiterated the misgivings he expressed in 1950.

> One of the things that made me unhappy at Strasbourg was that I saw that, at the first meeting, anyhow, of the Assembly, instead of trying to get co-operation and to provide organs of co-operation, there was an attempt to provide a full-blooded political constitution, that there were members there who were actually dividing themselves into socialist parties, and so on, as they might do in a national parliament. As far as we are concerned, whilst we wish well to all who think it is in their interest to do that, we certainly felt that we should not be committed as a nation to do it.

There would hardly be a more non-federalist attitude than this.

Seán MacBride, no longer in office but supporting the government, joined in the debate. Other speakers were Daniel Desmond (Labour), Declan Costello (Fine Gael) and Jack McQuillan, a colleague of Dr Noel Browne, who warned, more than once in the course of his speech, that 'as far as Ireland is concerned she should try and keep her nose out of the business of other nations and try and look after her own business first'. This did not elicit any Ministerial response.

As far as attitudes of non-politicians were concerned, the archives of the College of Europe in Bruges revealed a most interesting analysis of Irish attitudes in the form of a confidential report sent by M. Colin de Terrail, Secretary General of the French National Committee of the International Chamber of Commerce to Mr E. G. Thompson of the European Youth Campaign secretariat in Paris after the meeting in Athy in December 1953. In his covering letter M. Colin de Terrail warns that it was a fleeting visit and he does not pretend to sum up an entire country as the result of his experience but that he sends his impressions so that they might be added to others and the whole may provide an accurate picture. He was obviously touched by the warmth of his reception and impressed by the leadership of Macra na Feirme.

His report makes clear that he considered that Ireland felt herself closer to the Catholic countries of the European continent than to England or America. He believed that 'les élites Irlandaises' looked to Europe to act as a counterbalance to the close ties with Great Britain and that 'the Irish would rally without hesitation to the European Movement if its aims were solely cultural'.

> But they are political. In this respect Ireland is still more insular than England and public opinion is wary of countries which it knows nothing about and whose help will not be forthcoming to solve the only problem which interests it: the partition of Ireland between the Republic and the 'six counties' attached to the United Kingdom. The Irish representatives at the Council of Europe seem to look on themselves as observers there and it would appear inadvisable to try, for the moment, to get them to abandon this role.

He felt that the campaign for European union on economic lines would be more promising and that the Irish might well support the Strasbourg Plan which was designed to link the sterling zone with Western Europe. He outlined the problems of the Irish economy, notably lack of capital and equipment, and showed how Irish agricultural products were unable to be exported to the US while the Commonwealth as a whole produced a surplus of meat. It would therefore be in Ireland's interest to look to Europe both for investment and outlets.

1955–7

The addition of a United Nations Association (following the accession of Ireland to UN in 1955) to the many other bodies studying and promulgating all kinds of ideas and organisations in Dublin at this period did not take away from discussion of European questions. And 'Europe' was certainly not confined to the member countries of the Council of Europe. In June the rising of workers in Poznam reminded the Irish that Poland still had a problem which all the talk about 'resistance to . . . Communist power' was unable to help. Éamon de Valera, in opposition, is constantly reported on educational and human rights issues and there is a very full report of his speech on 'The Meaning of Human Rights' at an International Students' Seminar organised by the European Youth Campaign in University College, Galway and of the manner in which he answered the challenge of a Unionist member of the audience.[7] From de Valera, and other speakers at that time, there is a constant reminder that Europe has been cut in half and that at least part of the truncated piece is, by tradition or culture, part of the West rather than the East. The shock of the Hungarian rising in October 1956 and the brutality of its suppression made a change of attitude to the 'Cold War' inevitable. No longer did the United States appear as the saviour of anti-Communist forces. It had undoubtedly encouraged disaffection towards the Communist rulers of countries behind the 'Iron Curtain' but when the resistance took physical form neither the United States nor her allies in NATO were prepared to risk another world war to back up the cajolery of Radio Free Europe. Perhaps the reactions were too simple, too black and white. It would not have been in the interests of Europe, or Ireland, had there been a third world war as a result of Hungary.

The noises which began to emanate from Britain during 1956 reinforced the shift away from philosophical consideration of Europe's destiny to the more mundane issues of free trade. The introduction of petrol rationing in Britain after the Suez fiasco and the signs that the proposed European Economic Community was about to become a serious trade hazard for Britain and the Commonwealth prompted the idea of a 'free trade' association embracing most of Western Europe, with special provisions for the Commonwealth. The OEEC ended its second phase in 1956 and became embroiled in much more controversial, public and political bargaining. Procedures which had worked successfully in earlier years stagnated with disuse and it became obvious that the setting of 'intergovernmentalism' which was the basis of the Organisation, gave great power to states which were already strong, in a way which had not been so blatant in the negotiations for the European Coal and Steel Community. Economically weak countries, whose trade was not crucial to the system, played little real part in decision making. The fact that no parliamentary diplomacy was involved gave the major states even more power. In the OEEC the United Kingdom and France were able to play at diplomatic blackmail and block each other's moves, simply because they represented such a large slice of the other members' real and potential trade. Ireland possessed no such lever. The procedure of 'splitting the difference' disappeared when the economic stakes became too high and, in spite of the statements of Lemass and his officials, the unimportance of Ireland became painfully clear the following year.

It would seem[8] that 'the Six' were not regarded as a serious alternative by the Irish negotiators at that stage and they might well have tried to fall in with whatever free trade agreement finally came up had not the exclusion of agriculture made it quite impossible for Ireland to survive in a free-trade-minus-agriculture association. As long as there was even a faint chance that farm produce might be included they were prepared to soldier on and any pressure to look elsewhere came from a small group of economists, farm organisations and a few public figures but not from the civil service. The experience of the negotiations, however, made these same civil servants more sympathetic to the European Community when the time came.

The debate had developed along economic lines and hopes of a truly Continental union died away. The idea of cultural independence from Anglo-American domination, however, remained seductive, especially to Irish men and women who prided themselves on their liberation from the old love-hate relationship between Ireland and her big sister across the water.

Free Trade versus Common Market 1957–9

In retrospect, 1956 seems to have marked the lowest point of Ireland's economic and social achievement in the post-war period, but there were so many problems outstanding in 1957 that the year hardly started on a surge of optimism. The deflationary policy adopted by the government had reduced the balance of payments problem, but at the cost of holding back economic expansion.[1]

The refusal of Britain to join the Economic Community was surprising only to those who had taken Churchill's speeches when in opposition as firm commitments which would be honoured by a Conservative government in power. It is doubtful if Irish politicians or the Irish public ever expected British involvement in a political union as long as even the shades of Empire floated through the House of Commons. British refusal to join the EEC therefore upset no Irish apple-carts, but her proposal to create a new, bigger and looser alternative did hit the country just when it was trying to climb out of an economic trough.

There was good press coverage of Reginald Maudling's plans for a European Free Trade Area (EFTA), without any agricultural or political commitments, and the Irish Ambassador to Paris, William P. Fay, attended the OEEC negotiations on these lines and proposed a special working committee to study the agricultural problem. This suggestion was, not surprisingly in view of the implications of agriculture for all the member countries, agreed. Most Irish political energies were concentrated on the General Election held on 5 March, an election which brought Fianna Fáil back into power and returned three seats to Sinn Féin and one to 'Unemployed'. With de Valera back in office as

Taoiseach and Seán Lemass in his old post as Tánaiste and Minister for Industry and Commerce it might have been expected that Fianna Fáil would revert to its traditional policy of protection for Irish industry. In spite of a tough budget in May from Dr Ryan, the Minister for Finance, there were signs that official doctrines of economic policy were likely to change.

It is noticeable that from 1957 onwards, numerous references to the EFTA begin to crop up at annual dinners and annual general meetings (though there are almost none to the European Economic Community). Most bodies, or their officials, were concerned about the lack of information their organisation had on the free trade proposals or, more accurately, about the fog surrounding the government's policy regarding these proposals. On May 7 a memorandum entitled 'Ireland and the Free Trade Area' was issued by the government for 'the information of interested organisations and individuals'[2] and there is increasing evidence that the business and industrial sector was growing more and more concerned at the probable impact of European developments on the Irish economy.

In the earlier part of 1957 the Department of Finance had invited the views of the Board of the Central Bank as to 'whether it would be in Ireland's interests to join the proposed European Free Trade Area'.[3] It was apparently 'recognised by the Board that . . . much depended on the British attitude towards the exclusion of agricultural products from the scope of the arrangements'. The Board found that 'the disadvantages which would result from failure to join the proposed Free Trade Area were likely to outweigh the temporary adjustments necessary in our economy consequent on a decision to join'. The Governor elaborated on this view in a memorandum which he sent to the Secretary of the Department of Finance, T. K. Whitaker, and mentioned that staying outside 'would mean the erection of another barrier between Northern Ireland and ourselves'. The general message was that Ireland had little option but to try and join. The possibility of association with the European Community in some other way was not mentioned.

One of the best political discussions of the current problems came about through a motion, put down by John A. Costello, James Dillon and Liam Cosgrave in Dáil Éireann on 2 July 1957 asking the government to set up a 'select Joint Committee to enquire into the economic consequences for Ireland likely to follow the participation or non-participation of this country in the proposed Free Trade Area and the European Economic Community'.[4] Seán Lemass asked that it should not be put to a division because the government had practical and constitutional objections to such a committee. These objections disappeared when, many years later, it was decided to form an all-party committee of the Oireachtas to monitor the effects of EEC regulations on Irish legislation after Ireland's entry into the European Community.

John A. Costello explained his concern. 'I said it was a fact-finding commission, although I dislike that phrase, intended to educate Deputies who, I repeat again, know nothing whatever about the difference between the Common Market and the Free Trade Area. I am sure 99 per cent of Deputies and Senators are not properly informed of the issues and arguments involved.'[5]

Lemass dealt with the question in his best Delphic style. Having disagreed with the proposition, because of 'practical and constitutional difficulties' he went on to defuse the issue. He explained the three working committees which had been set up by the OEEC and their functions. Then he became positively magisterial.

> No sudden or radical change affecting our trade is about to take place. Indeed, the setting up now by the Dáil of such a committee as is proposed would give a wrong impression by conveying a suggestion of urgency that is not justified. . . . So far as the motion contemplates an examination of the desirability of joining or not joining the European Economic Community the idea is, I think, even more unrealistic.

Costello, in his reply at the end of the debate returned to the Tánaiste's denial of urgency. He warned that the very idea of a free trade area had been conceived in panic as a reaction to the speed with which the European Economic Community had come into being.

The motion was withdrawn in an amicable way, having at least achieved its secondary objective of raising the whole matter in the Dáil. Allowing for the exaggeration in Costello's figure of 99 per cent of the legislature ignorant of both Free Trade and the European Communities it is apparent that many deputies were anxious about the nature and scope of negotiations of which they knew very little. Clearly Seán Lemass was not going to reveal anything; he wanted to see the whites of the free traders' eyes before he would decide when to fire his shot – and in what direction. He was to follow up the circular mentioned by Costello with others in similar vein and he was not averse to fielding questions on the current negotiations within the OEEC. Non-Irish observers might be forgiven for surprise at the vigour with which the Irish government, and Seán Lemass in particular, was to pursue membership of the European Communities within three years.

In the interim, the meetings and discussions gathered momentum and by January 1958 Maudling was in Dublin for talks with Lemass and Patrick Smith, the Minister for Agriculture, on the British proposals. The press release was the usual anodyne description of a 'full and frank discussion'. A better picture of the current British attitude to the Irish position may be gleaned from an article in *The Statist* published the same week in which it was argued that

> Ireland's attitude seems to be one of refusing to accept that she will not get exceptional treatment. . . . The fact is that no expert appraisal has yet been made of the likely implications on individual Irish industries of a free trade area in which all participating countries would be treated equally . . .

and the writer goes on to deplore the effects of the 1932 Control of Manufactures Act.[6] On January 14 a memorandum was at last issued by the Department of Industry and Commerce on the present stage of Free Trade Area discussions, a memorandum which may have gone a little way towards meeting the many calls for more information.

Seán Lemass, keeping control of the issues in his own hands, issued a statement at the Free Trade Zone negotiating committee of OEEC saying that the British proposals on agriculture were too vague and gave a press conference on his return, which the *Irish Independent* carried under the banner, NO DECISIONS YET MADE. The Irish Association for Cultural, Social and Economic Relations held a symposium in Belfast on 10 February 1958 which was covered by all papers in the Republic. The Irish Association draws members from across the political spectrum and has two committees; one for members resident in Northern Ireland and one for members in the Republic. The presidency alternates North and South as does the annual conference. The main speaker was Seán Lemass and his theme was that the European Free Trade Area, if properly constructed, i.e., to include agriculture and the various safeguards proposed by Ireland, would benefit the North of Ireland.

The Council of Europe had become less important, in political terms, both to Europe and to Ireland but its increasing involvement in cultural and educational affairs, paradoxically, brought it nearer to many Irish people. In April 1958 the Minister for Education, Jack Lynch, was elected vice-president of the Consultative Assembly at Strasbourg, an event which shows the change of emphasis from the early days when de Valera sought election as president. The Irish political parties no longer used the Council for anti-partition platforms, nor for contentious political debates, and the OEEC had become the venue for tough economic and political bargaining but the Council of Europe remained a useful meeting place for maintaining contact with most of Western Europe and for promoting the kind of intellectual 'freedom of Europe' which was wistfully associated with the Golden Age of European culture.

Many Irish delegates had taken part in the work of committees and attended and spoke at the Assembly during the fifties. Declan Costello (who had been marked by Joseph Retinger as 'a coming man') played a positive role. In 1957 he complained that:

> No less than three separate European parliamentary assemblies have been created in recent years and only the prompt action of our President and some of our colleagues prevented the creation of a fourth. Defence, Coal and Steel production and economic affairs have now passed and are in the process of passing into the Assembly of the W.E.U. and the proposed Assembly of the E.E.C.[7]

He went on to express concern about the British Grand Design for an 'Atlantic Community', describing it as 'a vague and, I believe, dangerous chimera'.

Jack Lynch attended the Assembly in 1957 and became one of the vice-presidents in 1958, at a time when the Irish delegates were becoming more concerned with the possibility of being left out of both blocs should a final split come between the proposed EFTA and the existing EEC.

In spite of all the solid work being done, in the committees of the Council of Europe and the OEEC, and in the official and unofficial meetings of politicians and others and the optimistic noises which emanated from such sources it became clear by the end of 1958 that the Free Trade Area plans were running into very heavy weather and would probably founder. The heavy headlines 'AGRICULTURE MUST BE LINKED IN F.T. PLAN – IRISH VIEW ADOPTED – MR. LEMASS AT PARIS TALKS' in October 1958 looked more hopeful than the small print read. It was becoming more and more obvious that Britain would not budge on either agriculture or adequate control of competition and that 'the Six' would not jeopardise their hard-won unity for a twentieth-century version of the Manchester doctrine of free trade.

The European Economic Community began to operate in 1959; the opinion of most commentators was summed up by L. R. Murray in *The Irish Times,* 'Britain has suffered a serious defeat in her fight to set up a Free Trade Area to be linked with the Common Market'. Nevertheless politicians, particularly in Ireland and Britain, kept on trying to salvage something. Ireland was keenly aware of her vulnerable position if EFTA should fail. She could not afford to join Britain and the Scandinavians, thus permanently condemning Irish agriculture to the role of supplier of cheap food to Britain and opening the Irish market to competition from the most advanced industries in Europe. Nor was she prepared in any sense of the word, to cut herself off from the British market and throw in her lot with 'the Six'.

During a speech to the Dublin Chamber of Commerce Seán Lemass spelled out the reasons he continued to fight for a Free Trade Area which might be acceptable to both sides.

> It seems clear that if an agreement for a European Economic Association came into operation we could not afford to remain outside it but generally we conceive it to be in our interests in the present state of our economic development to seek to minimise the obligations we would in such an event have to undertake. Thus we find ourselves supporting the British conception although for very different reasons.[8]

There are signs elsewhere, however, that many sectors of the Irish community were making a serious, if somewhat belated, effort to make contact with European counterparts and organise themselves in readiness for some form of European association. The National Farmers Association joined the International Federation of Agricultural Producers (FIPA) in 1958, not a surprising move considering the long-standing interest of the agricultural community in European developments. The Federation of Irish Manufacturers set up a study-group on EFTA, also in 1958. In January 1959, an Irish section of the European Productivity Agency was formed to include representatives of the Federated Union of Employers, the Federation of Irish Industry, the Institute for Industrial Research and Standards, the trade unions and the universities.

The reconstituted Irish Council of the European Movement reflected the growing interest in the European arena; it now had among its members a high proportion of those involved in agriculture, industry and the economic life of the country. The former chairman, Dr Donal O'Sullivan, was elevated to the post of president and Dr Garret FitzGerald became chairman with Denis Corboy as active director of the Movement.

The history of 1958-9 reads like the report of an economic juggler trying to keep several plates whirling in mid-air until such time as he could decide which one to present with a flourish. During the winter and spring of 1957-8 the Department of Finance prepared a comprehensive survey of the economy, including its potential as well as its deficiency, and set out a set of proposals for future action. This was presented to the government in May 1958 and was published in November under the title of 'Economic Development' simultaneously with the First Programme for Economic Expansion which was largely based on the survey. This Programme laid emphasis on 'Grass before Grain' in the agricultural sector and put export-oriented expansion, even if foreign-owned, before dependence on protected domestic enterprise.

> It would be unrealistic, in the light of the probable emergence of a Free Trade Area, to rely on a policy of protection similar to that applied over the past 25 years or so. Assuming that a Free Trade Area is set up in Western Europe and that Ireland joins the Area, the Government will, of course, still be prepared, in suitable cases to grant protection to worthwhile new industries up to the limits permissible under the rules of the Free Trade Area.[9]

But the Free Trade Area talks collapsed and in May, Sweden, with backing from London, proposed the Stockholm Plan for an economic association of Seven: Great Britain, Norway, Denmark, Sweden, Finland, Austria and Portugal. Ireland appears to have been neither consulted nor invited to join and suddenly she found herself completely isolated with only her 1948 Trade Agreement with Britain to offer any protection for her exports.

It is not easy to plan economic development based on export-oriented industries if most of your exports are denied reasonably free access to their markets. There was a second shock in June 1959 when Britain offered considerable tariff concessions to Denmark (mainly to induce the Danes to throw in their lot with the Seven, since Denmark had extensive trading links with Germany and 'the Six'). Irish bacon producers would have to compete on equal terms with the Danes within two years and they were a long way from being able to do so. The Deputy Secretary-General of the OEEC told a meeting in Dublin in July 'You are now going to lose, probably forever, your privileged position on the UK agricultural market'.[10]

The government hurriedly sent a few more plates spinning. Application was made to the Commission of the European Community in Brussels to open diplomatic relations with the Community. Secondly, requests were sent to all the members of both the Six and the Seven to extend to Ireland, temporarily and unilaterally, all the tariff and quota concessions they were giving one another. (This was a piece of window-dressing, designed to keep Ireland in mind, since it was never remotely likely that either group would give such concessions to an outsider who was both economically and politically weak.) The Department of Finance was instructed to undertake initial studies on the implications of membership, associate and full, of EEC and EFTA. Thirdly, an Anglo-Irish Trade Committee was established to negotiate a new trade agreement with Great Britain.

The press of events ensured that the Anglo-Irish Trade Agreement was not completed until 1965 when conditions both in Ireland and Europe had considerably changed.

1959 marked some dramatic changes in Irish life. The first was the retirement from party politics of Éamon de Valera when he became President of Ireland and the succession of Seán Lemass to the post of Taoiseach on 23 June 1959, a post for which he had seemed destined for many years.

In September of the same year the two trade union congresses became one as the Irish Congress of Trade Unions and raised hopes, not only for continuing trade union unity, but also for the Labour Party since it could hope for a more solid relationship with a single Congress.

In his first news conference as Taoiseach, Seán Lemass announced an end to the term 'anti-Partition' in official statements about Northern Ireland. The main economic problems of the North were similar to those of the Republic and would yield to the same treatment; goodwill was the only possible policy, not coercion or force. A later press conference brought out the idea of a Customs Union or Free Trade Area between North and South and tripartite discussions between Ireland, Northern Ireland and Britain. There was no response from Northern Ireland however until after Lord Brookeborough's retirement as Prime Minister of Stormont in 1963.

There were other events which, in retrospect, were to have quite a deep effect on Irish life outside the political arena, north and south of the Border. One was the death on 9 October 1958 of Pope Pius XII. His successor, Pope John XXIII, was to change the accent of Catholicism in a manner which was to have an effect on Irish life, opening the door as it did to a greater respect for other religions and a more popular (its opponents might even say vulgar) approach to religious worship and practice.

While certain aspects of Irish political life might well support an outsider's popular view of the country as heavily Catholic and conservative, the economic structure, particularly in the period under review, reflected a pragmatic radicalism which suited the politicians and the country at the time. The opposition to 'continental-style' socialism was therefore reduced as soon as it was apparent that Italian and French Christian Democrats were prepared to cooperate with the Socialists and the tie between Communism and 'left-wing' became looser. As long as there was no talk of collective farms or state ownership of small holdings and businesses, the Irish public was prepared at least to look at what the Europeans had to offer and the change in the Vatican helped that general thaw.

The second non-political event which had an important effect on Irish attitudes, to Europe and to the rest of the world, was the decision to set up an Irish television station.

Television had been accidentally available to those living on the east coast of Ireland (which is the majority of the population) since the BBC and Independent Television strengthened their stations in Wales and Northern Ireland. A decision therefore had to be made as to whether or not such a situation should be allowed to continue indefinitely or an Irish service established. That decision was fairly easily made and in 1953 a committee was set up comprising Leon Ó Broin, Secretary of the Department of Posts and Telegraphs, T. J. Monaghan and Maurice Gorham, the then Director of Broadcasting in Radio Éireann to investigate and report on the implications (financial, technical and programming) of an Irish television service.[11]

The progress of events was leisurely, mainly because the economic plight of the country made television appear rather like Marie Antoinette's cakes, but the debate became hotter in the late fifties as the economic climate began to improve and a dramatic increase in Irish television-owners was noticed. In March 1958 a twenty-man Commission was set up to report within a year on proposals to set up a television service for Ireland.

Since Irish television broadcasting did not begin until 1961, its effects belong to a later period but the growing accessibility of British television, both BBC and Independent, had conditioned many Irish viewers to look for a considerable amount of their news and current affairs from television as well as newspapers. Had Radio Telefís Éireann not come into being when it did, Irish viewers would have had no counterbalance to British views of the European Communities. Nor would there have been any serious examination of Community proposals in relation to Ireland's political, economic and social position, and it is probable that there would have been a large anti-Common Market lobby, particularly in urban areas of Ireland.

Taking the Plunge 1960–61

The uncertainty in which the sixties began could not fail to affect Ireland. Yet the situation at home was rather more hopeful than it had been. 1960 was quite a good year economically, with a growth rate of four and a half per cent and though a wet harvest-time had a bad effect on agriculture, industrial exports, the balance of payments and savings all turned out better than had been anticipated.[1] At the same time The Netherlands and Belgium were in severe economic difficulties and the Economic Community experiencing teething troubles. Greek negotiations for associate membership of the Community were in trouble and the lesson was not lost on Ireland.

The climate had changed and it was apparent that while Ireland was still vulnerable she was no longer so much on the defensive as regards international opportunities and obligations.

Another pointer to changing times was the case brought by Gerard Lawless to the European Court of Human Rights in Strasbourg against the Irish Government arising from his internment.[2] This case attracted much attention at home and caused some comment in legal circles in Europe since Ireland was, at that time, unusual in allowing a private citizen to take action against the state in the European Court. The case in no way diminished the prestige of the Irish courts but it brought a European dimension to the sensitive area of human rights.

Irish public opinion adapted remarkably quickly to the new situation created by the failure of the Maudling proposals. Perhaps this was because they were fundamentally unfavourable to Irish conditions or because closer contact with the rest of Europe opened up new possibilities. In either case there is no doubt that the exclusion of Ireland both from the Six and the Seven left the country in a vacuum which neither the nation nor the government was anxious to accept as permanent. The political and social mood of the country was not as unprepared for the decision to apply for membership of the European Community which was announced in 1961 as some commentators seemed to think.

The General Election in 1961 was 'remarkable for the absence of controversy on entry into the Common Market or on general economic policy'.[3] There was no controversy because 'Free Trade' was never popular, never attractive in Ireland. It may have been a relief to Ireland to hear Britain look for membership of the European Communities (for in 1960 or 1961 she was certainly not prepared to look for entry without Britain) but the decision to look for full membership was an act of faith in the Irish economy which would have seemed like lunacy only ten years earlier. It is important to remember, however, that the change in the economists, the politicians, the bankers, the businessmen and the public was as great as the change in the economy itself. Political choice is made by men and women for reasons which have little enough to do with balance of payments figures and the man who can predict where and why a mood of confidence will cover a market will make his fortune several times over.

An important effect of the improved financial situation of Ireland from 1960 onwards was the decision by the Irish government, and its advisors, that a small, open economy had to decrease its dependence on its large neighbour and that Europe was the most realistic alternative. It is no harm to remember that there has always been freedom of movement for labour, capital and, on the whole, for goods between Ireland and Great Britain. Ireland was extremely vulnerable to changes of policy made in Westminster to suit British conditions but was powerless to influence them. The maintenance of a fixed exchange rate between the Irish pound and the pound sterling further increased the impact of British policy on Irish attempts to regulate incomes, prices and investments policy.

The similarities and distinctions between the economies of Ireland, North and South, from 1960 to the mid-seventies, are outlined in a collection of essays called *Economic Activity in Ireland – A Study of Two Open Economies*. In his contribution on 'The Foreign Sector', Dermot McAleese, discussing the transition from protectionism to free trade, states that

> For the Republic, entry into the EEC represented the culmination of a process which had begun in the mid-50s. Throughout this period, policies of protection and resistance to foreign ownership of companies in the Republic had been giving way to a new set of industrial policies which took the form of encouragement to exports through tax and marketing aids, the provision of grants to new industries (irrespective of the nationality of their owners), and the gradual dismantling of import barriers and restrictions.[4]

The tenth anniversary of the foundation of the Council of Europe, as we have seen, had been marked by a glowing tribute from the Minister for External Affairs to the Dáil in 1959. In his speech introducing the estimates for his Department, however, Frank Aiken concentrated on the United Nations and it was left to the opposition, particularly Fine Gael, to ask what policy the government had decided to adopt in the Free Trade negotiations. Indeed, James Dillon, with his customary flourish of rhetoric, worried about the division between the Six and the Seven which left 'the descaminados – Iceland, Turkey, Greece and Ireland . . . the ones who had nothing to offer anyone except outstretched hands. We do not belong in that company'.[5] In his reply the Minister ignored the queries about EFTA and the Six.

For the next two years there was a steady stream of parliamentary questions, usually directed to the Taoiseach, Seán Lemass, concerning the shifting groups in Western Europe and the government's policy as regards economic and, on occasion, political integration. On 2 March 1960 Deputy Russell asked specifically for a statement on Ireland's possible form of association with the European Economic Community. The Taoiseach replied:

> Among the questions at present under examination by the Government in connection with our external trade policy is that of our future relations with the European Economic Community. I am not in a position to say anything more on the subject at the present time.

James Dillon asked the Taoiseach to note the forbearance of the Opposition. Reply: 'I appreciate the forbearance which has been shown by the Opposition on this matter' and so the pavane came to a gracious close, without revealing to the House or the country anything further of the government's intentions.[6]

There was a slight ripple of interest for 'Europe watchers' when Aiken made his speech on the estimates for his Department for 1960-61, reporting on the transformation of the OEEC into the OECD and the advantages of including the US and Canada in the organisation. With regard to the EEC and EFTA, which could hardly be ignored in such a context, the Minister said:

> I do not propose to enter into the substance of these problems which have been fully explained in various statements by the Taoiseach. I should mention, however, that we are represented on the Committee on Trade Problems which met in Paris from 29-30 March last to discuss future trade relations between the European Economic Community and the European Free Trade Area.[7]

It is obvious that the Minister chose to consider the matter solely in terms of a trading agreement and not one of political or foreign policy with which he would concern himself.

After the summer recess the pattern continued. In October Deputy Russell asked if we had yet decided to open formal negotiations with the Common Market. In November the issue was raised in connection with the Irish negotiations to join GATT and in December Deputy Esmonde asked if we had contact with the newly-established EFTA Secretariat in Geneva. At various stages it was pointed out that Ireland had established a diplomatic mission to the European Communities and that the nature of the Free Trade Area was such that it did not lend itself to formal representation by those who were not members. The consistent response was that the government was not yet prepared even to discuss the implications of the alternatives which it was considering. In February 1961 Deputy Norton asked if there were any developments. The Taoiseach replied: 'I dealt with this situation in a speech which I made recently in which I said we do not expect any developments earlier than next year, and perhaps the year after'.[8]

Most of the speeches and statements referred to had not been made in the Dáil but in May 1961 the Taoiseach, pressed by Deputies Browne and McQuillan, who mentioned newspaper reports of developments in Britain, made a reasonably clear and important statement. Summarising the difficulties which had arisen in 1957-8 he showed that the OEEC had been unable to solve them.

> Until recently, the prospects of a link between Britain and the Common Market seemed slight. There have, however, been indications during the past few months that the British Government may be contemplating the possibility of entering the Common Market on certain conditions. It is the Government's view that, if Britain should take this step, we should *consider establishing a link* with the Common Market and endeavour to secure terms of membership or association which would satisfactorily take account of our economic circumstances.[9] (Italics mine.)

Several deputies tried to pursue the matter but he went no further.

In June 1961 Lemass was again questioned by Deputy Declan Costello, but on a slightly different line. Asked if it would be politically desirable to look for membership of the Community the Taoiseach replied:

> The factors which arise in connection with possible membership on our part of the European Economic Community are primarily of an *economic nature*. There are, as well, certain political implications which, in my opinion, are not such as to make it undesirable for this country to join the Community on the hypothesis mentioned by the deputy.[10]

The enthusiasm expressed in this double negative was unlikely to set the country alight. By the following week (21 June 1961) in response to nineteen questions, Lemass announced that he had decided to issue a White Paper on the whole issue but still considered it premature to express the government's opinion.[11] The opposition naturally took out their battering rams. The stone-wall stood. On 5 July 1961, subsequent to the publication of the promised (but disappointing) White Paper,[12] the Taoiseach issued the statement for which the country had been waiting. After outlining the situation and explaining that there were to be talks between the British and Irish Ministers for External Affairs and Finance and, of course, himself, Lemass continued: 'The Government have taken steps to inform each of the Six Governments of the European Economic Communities and the Commission of the Community in Brussels that, in the event of the United Kingdom applying for membership of the EEC, we also will so apply'.[13]

There was a slight procedural problem because ratification of the OECD was on the Order Paper and some speakers felt that the two issues were becoming confused but, on the whole, it was a long and thoughtful debate.

A careful analysis of the debate, and particularly of Lemass' own contribution, reveals three major factors in government policy towards the European Community which had not been previously spelled out – at least in the Dáil. The first, which comes as no surprise from politicians and their civil service advisors, was the determination not to abandon the British market for openings, however promising, in the rich pastures of the EEC. This attitude was to persist in spite of increasing difficulties for Ireland with the Anglo-Irish trading situation.

The second factor was the tacit acknowledgment that those engaged in agriculture, industry and the trade union movement would have to be involved in a way which had not arisen before. The Taoiseach announced that he had issued invitations to the different sectors of the economy to meet the relevant departments. This was probably due to a realisation that civil servants, no matter how competent, were not going to be able to lead those intimately involved in industry and agriculture from on high. Businessmen and farmers and trade unionists were making it clear that they wanted information – both on what was happening in Europe and on the possible options to Ireland – and they had become restive at the blanket silence which had heretofore met their questions. The direct involvement of those outside party politics and the civil service in the preparation for entry into the European Communities, which were highly politicised organisms, was a new development in Irish life and was to become more intense in later years. The pattern of using producers' organisations, the professions or the trade unions as a stepping stone to national political life was an old one. The practice of openly consulting and informing those engaged in the economy of the course of international negotiations was new in 1961. It was brought about by pressure from within and without. From within because so many important organisations throughout the country were calling for the new approach, and from without because the pressure of events called for a stronger 'back-up' service of information and a wider consensus on policy than the official negotiators could muster without the active support of all sectors of the Irish community.

The third factor which emerged was the government's decision to look for full membership. Seán Lemass was challenged that he had seemed to favour association and the White Paper certainly emphasises the term 'link' to describe Ireland's probable relationship with the European Communities (and 'link' is a mild term for full membership of a Community with such intimate connections between its members). The Taoiseach denied that he had given this impression, or that the White Paper was less than full and factual. Is full membership consistent with the use of the word 'link'? Possibly, insofar as any one organ of the body could be described as being 'linked' to another, but in any case the Taoiseach's previous replies down the years had been so non-committal that any interpretation could fit. And the White Paper, for all its breadth and optimism, shows the signs of hasty preparation in its lack of analysis and detailed information. No doubt it can be argued that the Paper was confined to 'facts', that figures were scarce and that every sector was at least mentioned. Since 1959, however, it had become quite clear to many in Ireland that membership of the Community was at least a possibility and better preparation, at least on paper, might have been expected. As far as 'factual' is concerned, it is debatable that a document which fails to explain the political dynamics of the Communities under discussion is an adequate guide for entry into their activities. What would have happened had Ireland and the United Kingdom been accepted as members in 1961 or 1962?

The Taoiseach's own speeches, moreover, represent some difficulty for those attempting to analyse his policy because so many of the most important were made, not in the Oireachtas, but to meetings and conferences throughout the country and for these the only reports extant are from newspapers. His example was followed by the other members of his government. A dramatic front-page headline in *The Irish Times*[14] for example asks, WILL IRELAND JOIN 'THE SIX'? and carries the report of a speech by Dr Ryan, Minister for Finance, to a meeting of An Comh-Chomhairle (a discussion group under the auspices of the Fianna Fáil Party) in Dublin, in the course of which he pointed out that European nations were moving rapidly towards lower tariff and freer trade and went on to say, 'We may be compelled to take big and dramatic decisions sooner than we would decide to do of our volition'. The reporter comments that this may have been related to the recent visit of Christopher Soames, the British Minister for Agriculture, to Dublin, which had taken place earlier in May.

Dr Ryan's remarks were soon followed by what was often referred to as Lemass's 'Killarney' speech. This was addressed to the Irish Management Institute on 12 May 1961 and was carried by all the papers, and by Radio Éireann. In it the Taoiseach made a major survey of the needs of Irish industry and the problems of functioning in a small economy. He then went on to the meat which his audience and a sizeable part of the country at large had been waiting for.

> The Government would like to see in a number of industries – in the light of an expected intensification of competition in home and export markets – the advantages of rationalisation of competition in home and export markets. For the Government's part, we accept an obligation to help in getting that operation started wherever there is a desire to start it.

This was a clear warning but hardly a definition of government policy on the precise arrangement it would seek between the European Economic Community and Ireland and it was not surprising that an *Irish Times* report of the Clann na Poblachta Ard Fheis of 1961 in Athlone should carry the heading SAY YES OR NO TO COMMON MARKET.[15] It reports a resolution which 'viewed with concern the Government's delay in formulating and declaring its policy as to Ireland's participation in the European Common Market'. Seán MacBride was reported as having said that while Britain had now decided, we should have known and prepared ourselves for the past five years for membership. MacBride made it clear that he favoured full rather than associate membership; his words reflected a growing impatience with the mixture of exhortation and generalities being issued by the government.

As Irish readers saw it, the British government, by contrast with their own, made most of its important announcements to the nation through the House of Commons. The Irish papers of 14 June 1961 quote the speech of the Prime Minister, Harold Macmillan, in the House of Commons in which he revealed that Duncan Sandys was to head a Ministerial team to consult the Commonwealth about Britain's joining the Six. *The Irish Times* interpreted this move as delaying Britain's membership by twelve months.

Lemass's next major speech on this topic was to the National Convention of Junior Chambers of Commerce in Ireland meeting at Shannon Airport. The headlines read: WHAT IRELAND MUST MEET ON JOINING E.E.C. – TAOISEACH EXPLAINS ISSUES[16] and Lemass pointed out that in Ireland discussions about the EEC had been largely confined to the question of trade and the implications of the European Community on trade.

He went on to outline the Rome Treaty and continued:

> It is not believed that political unity will grow automatically from economic unity; rather it is believed that it is only on the basis of political agreement that a permanent solution of the economic problem can be founded. . . .
>
> If we go into the E.E.C. we must have a view-point about this conception of economic unity and the political motives from which it derives, and we must have given thought to all its implications for the future of our country. . . .

The Taoiseach then examined the Assembly, the Council, the Commission and the Court of Justice:

> I have no desire to minimise the many and various problems which accession to the Rome Treaty in any form or manner must involve for this country, but the problem of remaining aloof must also be in the forefront of our thinking. It is a choice between two sets of problems and there is no easy decision.

This major, marathon speech shows Seán Lemass in his best political form. He was alleged to be blunt and he was certainly forthright on this, as on many other occasions, but the most careful analysis of what he says will reveal just how many options he contrived to leave open for his own negotiations. If he was to be refused full membership (which was a possibility) he had not slammed the door on association. If the negotiations were to drag on or be postponed he could remind his critics that he had warned of the problems and the delay might be a blessing in helping Ireland to equip herself to deal with them. If Britain went in quickly (i.e., within two years) and Ireland was also accepted, he had prepared the way by warning of the political and economic implications of membership of the European Community. If negotiations broke down irretrievably, the Taoiseach could justifiably claim that the 'many and serious' problems which accession would entail for Ireland would have been more than we, or the Community, could solve anyway. It was not the attitude of a Robert Schuman or Paul Henri Spaak but this approach, pragmatic and cautious, towards accession to the European Community shows some basis for the eventual alliance of Fianna Fáil and the Gaullists in the European Progressive Democrats.

The British government placed Edward Heath, the Lord Privy Seal, at the head of its negotiating team for entry into the EEC, which was a wise choice. Heath was not responsible for the problems left behind by the insensitivity of his Free Trade Area colleagues, nor for the difficulties created by the fact that four years of operation had stiffened the attitude of the Six original members, particularly the French. Seán Lemass put the Minister for Industry and Commerce, Jack Lynch, and the Minister for External Affairs, Frank Aiken, on the Irish team but seems to have kept a more personal involvement in developments than did his British counterpart.

The slowness with which the negotiations got under way jeopardised a successful conclusion. The autumn meetings were little more than a ritual taking up of positions on the British and Community sides and real negotiations were not begun until the settlement of the common agricultural policy had been made in January 1962 and the Community had entered the second phase of its development as laid down by the Treaty of Rome. The second half of 1961 was therefore fallow as far as Irish developments were concerned. The story of the stops and starts of negotiations belongs to another study.

Part Two

The Media

Since there was no Irish television until 1962, newspapers and radio were the two most significant branches of the mass media in the country. They reached the largest number of people and they were the vehicles for the greatest volume of information. They serve as a barometer of the rise or fall in importance in the public mind of any particular issue.

The Newspapers

Irish newspapers shared the problems of shortage of resources and money faced by the press in Europe in the immediate post-war years.

The three Dublin-based national papers had the advantage of a good distribution network and a solid nucleus of faithful readers throughout the country but they suffered from two disadvantages not felt by many of their Western European counterparts. The first was a heavy dependence on news agencies for coverage of outside events; second, the fact that they were English-language papers meant that the agencies supplied material which was written mainly for their powerful British customers. It was an inevitable consequence, rather than any sinister plot, that news stories about European developments concentrated on the repercussions on Britain and the Commonwealth. This dependence on outside sources for foreign news is noticeable in other ways too. Many important events have different headlines in the three papers but are followed by an identical text.

The creation of The Irish News Agency (INA) by the Inter-Party Government in 1948 was an attempt to break the paper wall surrounding Ireland. In theory the INA was set up to ensure an accurate flow of information in and out of the country. In practice, however, its destiny was linked to that of Seán MacBride who, as Minister for External Affairs, was responsible for its inception. It was he who appointed its first directors and he seconded one of his officials, Conor Cruise O'Brien, to run it. The INA became associated in many minds with the anti-partition policy of MacBride and with the politics of the Inter-Party government.

The Agency was organised into news, photographic and features departments and was linked internationally with the United Press service. It was never very popular with the Irish newspapers. In July 1957 it was closed down under a Fianna Fáil government, on grounds of economy, although it is difficult to see how it could ever have been judged as a money-making or even a self-financing operation. Its justification lay in its effectiveness as a means of communication between Ireland and the English-speaking world. In the early years it concentrated its news service in particular on events relating to Northern Ireland but by 1957, under the direction of Brendan Malin, it had broadened its scope, and its coverage of European developments in general was matched by a varied picture of Irish life sent out through its news and features divisions.

The second disadvantage suffered by the Irish dailies was competition from the big English popular papers. The popularity of English mass-circulation papers is relevant, not only because it affected the revenue and influenced the style of the Irish press but also because it meant that the Irish readership was being told about the world outside as seen through British eyes. The special 'Irish' editions were designed to avoid Irish censorship, to adopt a more respectable image and cover Irish sporting events, rather than offer political or economic interpretations of news which had a bearing on Irish conditions.

There was naturally great interest in the conflict between Russia and the United States and its European repercussions during the forties and early fifties. The Communist take-over of Czechoslovakia in February 1948 was fully covered in all the Irish papers and editorials and articles reflect the fear of Russian expansion and a new conflict in Europe. This was explicitly stated in the St. Patrick's Day speech by the Taoiseach, John A. Costello (fully reported in all papers) in which the keynote was in the opening, 'while our thoughts are with our own people we do not forget the sufferings of countless people in a continent wrecked by war and shattered by peace . . . .'.

All three papers carried weekly or occasional columns to offset the dearth of local Irish interest in the reports from Reuter and United Press. There were *The London Letter, The Paris Letter* (signed by Desmond Ryan), *The Way of the World* by Kees van Hoek. *The Irish Times* occasionally used the Guardian Service and Alistair Cooke's dispatches from America to supplement the ration. The appointment of Seán MacBride as Minister for External Affairs in 1948 and his obvious, active involvement in European affairs also brought at least some of the momentous affairs in the headlines a little nearer home. The reports on the signing of the statute of the newly formed Council of Europe in St James's Palace, carried on 6 May 1949, at least included a quotation from the Irish Minister on his hopes for the new institution, though the banner headlines in *The Irish Times* read COUNCIL OF EUROPE – CHURCHILL NOT A DELEGATE. Lest it be thought, however, that Europe loomed over-large on the horizon it should be pointed out that the main news story of May in that year was the implications of the 'Ireland Bill' and that there was the normal, annual, extensive coverage of the Feis Ceoil and the Spring Show.

The front pages of *The Irish Press* and *The Irish Times* and the main page of the *Irish Independent* on 11 August 1948 reported MacBride's decision to introduce the question of the partition of Ireland into the Council of Europe and discussed the forthcoming election of a president for that body. There were full reports from Strasbourg on the debates on the Cultural Committee reports and on the proposals for a European Convention of Human Rights and *The Irish Press* showed where its heart was in the headline, DE VALERA ABSTAINS IN VOTE AT STRASBOURG.

The official proposals made by the French government that France and Germany should place coal and steel under a single High Authority and invite others to join were prominently reported in all papers on 9 May 1950, but no particular comment was made. Throughout the first half of that year the main concerns were fear of a trade war, in addition to the continuing problems in Cyprus, China, the Middle East and Europe.

The headline of *The Irish Times* of 1 January 1951, U.S. END STATE OF WAR WITH GERMANY, puts the negotiations for the ECSC into the perspective in which they appeared to Irish readers. President Truman was to ask the US Congress to declare an end to the state of war but 'The declaration would fall short of an actual peace treaty' according to the AP text. Of the forty-seven states still technically at war with Germany, some thirty had indicated willingness 'to welcome Germany back into the Community of Nations'. *The Irish Times* published the British Honours List and all papers reported the current bank strike, rail strike, unusually bad weather, the appointment of a Prices Advisory Council and the announcement of a prices' freeze, plus the war in Korea. Later in the month there was a report of the visit of R. W. C. Mackay, MP, to Dublin to discuss with the government and Irish members of the Council of Europe the work of the Council of Europe committee set up to draft proposals to amend the Statute of the Council so that it might have some legislative authority. There was also full coverage, though no comment, on the French invitation to West Germany, Britain, Norway, Iceland, Denmark, Belgium, Luxembourg, Holland, Italy and Portugal to form a common European Defence Army, with a single responsible Minister. The problems of unemployment, inflation and political unrest were of much more immediate concern, and these continued throughout 1952 (and were underlined by the strike which put the national dailies off the streets from 12 July to 30 August 1952).

Between 21 February and 25 February there are several references to the Paris meeting called to draw up a project for a 'European Community'. It is apparent that the proliferation of assemblies and Councils of Ministers was causing confusion not only in the public mind but also leading to extreme fatigue in those expected to attend and report them. The pressure experienced in the sixties for a single European parliament for the European Communities was reminiscent of the concern felt by the leaders of the Six during the fifties at the increasing number of European organisations and communities. It may also explain why leader writers and correspondents largely neglected those bodies which, they felt, were becoming too numerous and complicated to explain to the reading public.

The coverage of the European Movement was as erratic as the progress of the Movement itself. The institution of the Movement at the Congress of Europe in The Hague in 1948 was fully covered by all papers and *The Irish Times* and *The Irish Press* both carried pictures of Winston Churchill attending. The *Irish Independent* carried an editorial on 8 May 1948 under the heading of CONGRESS OF EUROPE.

> There can be nothing but praise for efforts to give peace, stability and security to a continent which has already undergone terrible agony. When, however, examination is made of some of the aims of the Congress doubts may arise. A complete federation, a European Parliament, common citizenship, a single Defence Force, unified economy, common currency and removal of all customs barriers cannot be brought about without sacrifice of national sovereignty on the part of members of the federation. . . .

In spite of the headlines and photographs there was no mention of the delegation from Ireland, and when the Congress met again in The Hague in October 1953 the Irish papers ignored the event. The formation of the Irish Council of the European Movement (ICEM), however, was carried in a snippet on the front page of *The Irish Times* on 12 January 1954, though not by any other paper.

Throughout the next few years there is small but consistent coverage of events sponsored by the ICEM or by the European Youth Campaign, on a par with the coverage of many of the social and educational voluntary organisations which flourished throughout the period.

The final rejection of the ill-fated EDC was fully reported on 31 August 1954, but the main preoccupations of that autumn were the request that Six County MPs should have a right of audience in the Dáil, shooting in Northern Ireland, baby-snatching in Dublin, Cardinal Mindzenty and the debate in the British Labour Party between Attlee and Bevan about German rearmament. The Messina Conference at which the Foreign Ministers of the Six passed a resolution to set up the European Economic Community and Euratom was reported on 3 June 1955, but although material was now coming from UP and the Irish News Agency, there was still little or no background reported with an obvious bearing on the Irish situation.

Economic developments were overshadowed by the Hungarian rising and the Israeli/British/French invasion of Egypt in 1956 and these two events and their aftermath dominated editorials, features and news throughout the year.

The repercussions of the Messina conference were making themselves felt at second-hand by 1957. British reaction had been to propose the quite different idea of a Free Trade Association and 'Free Trade' had an ominous ring to Irish ears, particularly when coming from across the Irish Sea. Not surprisingly the papers report that the Federation of Irish Manufacturers was calling for consultation with the Government over European developments on 1 February 1957 and the *Irish Independent* of the same date carried a report from the Taoiseach that, 'the attitude that this country should adopt towards the proposals for a E.F.T.A. is at present being considered by the Government'. However discreetly the government, and indeed the political parties generally, were handling the matter, others were calling for positive reaction and the debate about where Ireland's interests lay had obviously begun.

Alderman G. Russell, Mayor of Limerick, was calling for 'deliberate and careful study of the proposed Free Trade Block for Western European countries';[1] a resolution was passed that 'Ireland Should Join the European Free Trade Area' at the Kings' Inns.[2]

There were two subsidiary reasons why the debate on European economic integration should suddenly become a feature of Irish current affairs. The first was increasing contact with the European mainland, whether as a result of trade, tourism or a conscious effort to improve direct links with the outside world. The Irish papers noted the new Aer Lingus flights to Dusseldorf, Brussels, Frankfurt, Zurich and Rome due to come into operation during the summer of 1957 and reported increased traffic on the Dublin-Paris route.

The second factor contributing to the interest was the fact that Seán Lemass, as Minister for Industry and Commerce when Fianna Fáil came back into power in March 1957, became involved in the OEEC negotiations concerning EFTA and it was Lemass, rather than Aiken or de Valera, whom the commentators watched during this period. From November 1957 until 1959 the newspapers present OEEC negotiations as seen through the eyes of Seán Lemass.

On 18 November 1957 the front pages of all papers have Lemass back from OEEC Committee of Ministers' Meeting and saying that a free trade pact would, after all, include farm products and that negotiations were 'as satisfactory as might be expected'. On 17 January 1958 Lemass issued a statement at a Free Trade Zone Negotiating Committee of the OEEC that the British proposals on agriculture were too vague and likely to be unacceptable. The following day there is an account of a press conference, given on his return with headlines, NO DECISIONS YET MADE. By 23 October 1958 *The Irish Press* main headline sums up the position: AGRICULTURE MUST BE LINKED IN F.T. PLAN – IRISH VIEW ADOPTED – MR. LEMASS AT PARIS TALKS. Reports were carried in all papers that a Free Trade Area could not exist on industrial products alone.

By 1959 all three Dublin papers were sending special correspondents to cover important international events abroad, more Irish organisations and politicians were giving press conferences and the papers were bigger, with more space for comment as well as news.

It was argued that it was the sea around the British Isles, rather than the border around Northern Ireland, which affected the vision of most Irish politicians, trade unionists and businessmen, but the Irish press could not be blamed for the lingering myopia. Perhaps the prose in 1960 was a paler shade of purple than that which blossomed in the forties and the leaders had become both shorter and slightly less thunderous but a reasonable proportion of the fatter editions were devoted to serious attempts to explain the important issues which had come up on the Irish horizon.

Radio Éireann

Radio Éireann has traditionally held a unique, if rather unenviable, place in Irish life. It was always short of money and constantly reproached for neglecting the wealth of talent which was popularly supposed to lurk in every town and barony in Ireland. It had to exist in the giant shadow of the BBC and, because of its limited hours of broadcasting, it knew its listeners had to depend on the other station for most of their music, entertainment and news comment. Maurice Gorham, a former Director of Radio Éireann, sums up the problem in his book on the history of the station.

> Radio Éireann was expected to do a great many things that were not demanded of other national radio services, most of them far better equipped. . . . It was expected to revive the speaking of Irish; to foster a taste for classical music; to revive Irish traditional music, to keep people on the farms . . . .[3]

The station began to expand in 1948. There was an increase in the number of licences, hours were extended and more professional staff recruited.

In 1951 Erskine Childers became Minister for Posts and Telegraphs and, as such, responsible for Radio Éireann. As a former journalist he was anxious to free the broadcasters from the restrictions of the civil service (their previous status) and improve the quality of broadcasting. Unscripted discussions on controversial topics were to be allowed and 'The Week in Leinster House' was a first attempt at consistent reporting of the proceedings of the Oireachtas. In 1952 a morning news programme was introduced and the appointment, as director, of Maurice Gorham, formerly a distinguished member of the BBC in 1953, increased the prestige and expanded the freedom of the station.

There is a certain difficulty in obtaining records of programmes dealing with international and European affairs prior to 1960 since there were few programmes dealing with current affairs, and those were live and not kept on tape. There are, however, two recordings in the 'Diary of the Year' series for 1950 and 1951 which give a good idea of what was considered important enough to include in the annual retrospective review. In the 1950 'Diary of the Year', actual fanfares announce the declaration of the signing of the Treaty of Rome by Robert Schuman. The reporter becomes lyrical in his enthusiasm.

> This was more than news – it was history . . . it signalled the beginning of a new order under which war between the two countries (Germany and France) would become impossible. . . . This was idealism wedded to realism . . . an attempt to bring about some peace and the social advancement of the citizens of the member states through economic co-operation and social advancement, beginning with the industries of coal and steel.

There is further mention of European affairs when Seán MacEntee's efforts to get certain rights written into the European Charter of Human Rights (notably the right to free elections and the right of parents to decide the education of their children) were reported. The resolution was accepted by the Committee of the Assembly of the Council of Europe but rejected by the Council of Ministers. This rejection was regarded by the Assembly as an emasculation of the Charter of Human Rights.

In the 1951 'Diary of the Year' an account of the celebrations of the anniversary of the Swiss town of St. Gall was followed by a relevant history lesson in the local high school. Éamon de Valera attended the celebrations and spoke in Irish at the library, which he commended to all serious students of Irish. Later on the mood changes and there is an extract from a speech made by Seán MacEntee, TD, in the Council of Europe, in which he declares that a people like the Irish who have 'recently recovered their liberties will not be willing to cede them – even in the face of grave peril' and records his support for Sir David Maxwell-Fife (British Conservative) who had earlier in the debate opposed any attempt at political union for Europe which would include Britain.

The next year with a significant European content was 1957 when the commentator dealt at length with the implications of a speech made by Seán Lemass in Dublin in December 1956 in which he had said that 'it is now almost certain that negotiations will be successful' for European free trade and that he expects the agreement would be signed by January 1961. The commentator gave the speech itself a big build-up talking about 'the dream that was at hand . . . the dream of a Europe without frontiers . . .'. There were no fanfares. There was also an extract from a speech by Dr A. Esmonde, TD, in the Council of Europe (October session) in which he sees 'in the free trade of Europe an opportunity for us . . . to sell not only our agricultural goods but our whiskey (slight laughter), tweeds, glass . . .' and his view that Ireland looked for further trade with Europe to improve her position of over-dependence on the British market. He was followed by a Danish representative who supported him and went on to say that 'Europe has to unite if she is to survive'. This was, in turn, followed by further extracts from another Lemass speech, trying to rouse Irish business into action. 'We cannot go out for great opportunities on a "limited liability" offer . . . we must get ourselves in shape'.

It is worth noting that Radio Éireann broadcast certain important speeches of Seán MacBride on European affairs in toto in 1949. Seán Lemass's speech in 1961, delivered in Killarney, in which he set out the government's views on Free Trade and the European Economic Community and the decision to seek membership of the Community, was also broadcast in full.

The programme which devoted most time to Irish-European affairs was 'Round Table on World Affairs', produced by Frank MacManus, which went out on Thursday evening. The most frequent contributors during the fifties were Dr Donal O'Sullivan (lecturer in International Affairs in TCD and chairman of the Irish Council of the European Movement), Professor Desmond Williams, Erskine Childers Junior and Vincent Grogan. The chairman was Jack White, then with *The Irish Times* and the regular contributors were often joined by Brian Cleeve, Professor John O'Meara, Donal Nevin, Dr T. McLaughlin, Kevin B. Nowlan, Garret FitzGerald, Seán MacBride, Dr S. Ehler, Senator Eoin Sheehy Skeffington, Peadar O'Curry, Lord Killanin, Professor Thomas Nevin, Sean Flanagan, TD, R. J. P. Mortished, Miriam Hederman, Donal O'Donovan, Col. Dan Bryan, Brian Farrell and occasional foreign visiting journalists.

'Farmers Forum' under Michael Dillon and Patrick O'Keeffe also dealt in passing with European markets and particularly the Green Pool and was another reflection of the interest of the agricultural sector in European affairs.

From 1956 onwards there is increasing emphasis on the debate about the effects of free trade on Ireland. On 13 February 1957 'Round Table on World Affairs' discussed 'European Free Trade' with Vincent Grogan, Garret FitzGerald and James J. Byrne.

During 1958 a fifteen minute series of comments, 'News Talks', was introduced after the 6:30 pm news on Sundays, edited by Michael McDonagh. These were short, scripted contributions on items which had occurred during the previous week and were unusual in that they came under the mantle of the News Section of Radio Éireann rather than that of Features. Another programme which marked an innovation in broadcasting was the thirty-minute 'Aer Iris' by Proinsias MacAonghusa which extended Irish language coverage of political personalities and events.

There were other programme series which lasted a few months and provided quite an amount of adult education, civics, debate and current affairs in a reasonably palatable form. These, and many of the other programmes mentioned earlier, owed a great deal to Francis MacManus, the director of Features in Radio Éireann. They contributed to the publicising of the European institutions which the Irish people were to be committed to join.

External Affairs information bulletins

The sealed archives of government departments are as frustrating to researchers as they are to newspapermen, but other sources of information are often overlooked despite the fact that they are available and were indeed intended for public reference. The Department of External Affairs information bulletins, which were sent to Irish Missions abroad and sometimes to news agencies and foreign press, changed title and format over the years. The name for most of the period under examination was *Éire/Ireland* with the sub-heading 'Information Bulletin'. These bulletins reflect the changing political, economic and social climate and, of course, the personality of their anonymous editors in the Department of External Affairs. The first, insistent, note struck is the constant anti-partition propaganda kept up from 1949 until the mid-fifties. Sir Basil Brooke is watched like a vulture, any publication or association which comes out against the partition of Ireland is quoted approvingly and any speech of any Irish politician dealing with the wrongs and injustice of the situation (and there were many) seems to be included. The second aspect which emerges is the remarkable diversity of subjects covered. Horse-breeding, racing and show-jumping are natural themes but coverage is given to health statistics, music, drama, the arts in general, scientific research, learned publications, farming, the GAA, rugby and other sports, industry, tourism and the development of peat. The third facet is the chronicle of diplomatic appointments, events, changes of government, and the reports of speeches of Irish Ministers to various international bodies, in particular the Organisation for European Economic Co-operation, the Council of Europe and, eventually, the United Nations.

The bulletins of the Department of External Affairs also highlight events in Ireland considered worthy of interest for those outside the country. There is, for instance, a brief account of the visit to Ireland of 'J. R. Colin de Terrail, Secretary General of the French Committee of the International Chamber of Commerce, (who) recently lectured on "The Economic Aspect of European Unity" at a week-end study seminar held in Athy, Co. Carlow (sic) by the European Youth Campaign for members of Macra na Feirme, the Irish Young Farmers' Organisation'[4] and a mention of the foundation of an Irish Council of the European Movement.[5]

As far as European affairs are concerned it can be said that there are three main strands in the Bulletins over the years. The first is the quotation, unfortunately without exact references to dates of publication, of extracts from European publications of items which reinforce the idea of Irish importance in European affairs. Secondly, there are reports of Irish involvement in the Council of Europe, the OEEC, and various private European cultural and political associations. Thirdly, there are political and economic speeches on Irish policy concerning European affairs. Since many of these were made not in the Oireachtas but at various gatherings throughout the country, and abroad, their inclusion is a valuable check on current newspaper reports which are, inevitably, edited and abbreviated.

Three speeches quoted by the Bulletin relating to other European developments for different reasons, deserve special note. The first is a text of a broadcast given by Frank Aiken, Minister for External Affairs on Radio Éireann on 5 May 1959 to mark the Tenth Anniversary of the establishment of the Council of Europe. Having outlined the role and history of the Council of Europe, Aiken went on to deplore the absence of countries from Eastern Europe from the Assembly and to explain that the Council worked 'towards a real union, not a monolithic structure in which national diversities of tradition and culture would be obliterated, but a genuine community of ideals and interests'. He then dealt with the criticism that the Council of Europe had no real powers. Such a criticism ignores the length of time it took democracy to develop within the member states. 'To jeopardise this unusual experiment in international relations by an undue haste would be both foolish and rash.'

> . . . such ambitious schemes as the European Payments Union, the Coal and Steel Community and the Common Market can fairly be said to have received their first impulsion from the debates in the Consultative Assembly.

The speech is obviously routine, bland and unexceptional. But it was made on radio, directly to the people and it can therefore be reasonably claimed that it reflects the message that Aiken wanted to convey. Which might fairly translate as: Europe has not the grandeur of the world scene which we play on in the United Nations, but it is where we live. The Council of Europe is useful so we use it and wish it well. But do not ask for too much too quickly. Aiken was no federalist.

The other two speeches date from 1961, after the decision had been made to seek membership of the European Economic Community. The first is that of Jack Lynch, then Minister for Industry and Commerce, speaking to a paper on the EEC read by the Auditor of the Historical Society of Trinity College, Dublin and reported, in extenso, in *Éire/Ireland.*[6] The Minister began by outlining the negotiations of 1956–8 to create a free trade area and described the result of the failure of negotiations to reconcile the two blocs which resulted.

> We had all along felt a certain sympathy with the European Economic Community and with the wider objectives at which it aimed. Having regard, however, to the great importance for our export trade of the British market, it would clearly not be in our interest to come

> to any arrangement which would disrupt our special trading relations with Britain . . . as would happen if we were to join the Common Market without Britain's doing so.

There follows a short passage to prove Ireland's record as a 'good European through history' and her record of membership of other organisations. Mr Lynch mentioned the obligations in the Treaty of Rome which related to the elimination of export controls, the free movement of workers, the right of establishment and others 'but there is no reason to anticipate that they will present any insuperable difficulty for us. . . . We cannot, in any event, take out of the Treaty and apply to ourselves only those parts which suit us particularly and leave the other parts. We must look at the Treaty as a whole and strike a broad balance'.

> . . . There can be no doubt about Ireland's sincere desire to play a full part in the attainment of this ideal. As the Taoiseach has said, this European Economic Community is a great conception fraught with immense possibilities for the future of Western Europe and indeed for all mankind and of such historical significance that many would wish to support it, even if it seems likely to create serious problems for their own countries and produce many short-term disadvantages.

Finally, a slightly earlier issue of the same year[7] covered the press conferences given by the Taoiseach, Seán Lemass, after his meeting with British ministers in London on 18 and 19 July 1961 to discuss relations between the two countries in the light of membership of the EEC. The meetings with Macmillan and the other ministers were confidential, so Lemass confined himself to general questions. He confirmed that Ireland saw no connection between NATO and membership of the EEC and mentioned that the sharing of sovereignty implied in the Rome Treaty had been discussed. In answer to a question on the implications for the unity of Ireland, Lemass replied:

> There is no doubt that the economic development problems of North and South (in Ireland) are fundamentally identical. These problems will become increasingly obvious in the context of the European Economic Community. The same questions are being asked in North and South and there is the same desire to get information so as to answer these questions.

He added that a meeting with Northern Ireland Ministers to discuss mutual problems might be useful later but it was still too soon to expect contacts of that kind. The tone and tenor of the report are light years away from the speeches made, admittedly never by Lemass, only five years earlier. The changed attitude to Europe reflects quite a few other changes which had taken place along the way.

The European Voluntary Organisations and the Universities

There is a strong tradition of voluntary organisations in Ireland; they are part of the fabric of social history, but their records are often scanty or non-existent and, occasionally (owing to efficient public relations or the presidency of a newsworthy personality at some period) they seem to have exerted greater influence than was actually the case. Membership figures are notoriously difficult to ascertain and can be meaningless. Is the fact that the Irish Countrywomen's Association, for example, was a member of the European Youth Campaign an indication that most of its members were aware of the EYC and supported its aims? And if not most, then how many? Fifty per cent, a quarter, a tenth, a few clubs, the Executive of the ICA, the members of the Executive who were representatives on the Executive of the EYC? It probably varied from year to year and from organisation to organisation.

Because, however, such organisations represent the work of the dedicated and because they exert a genuine influence they cannot be ignored in any serious study of the attitudes of the community in which they operate.

The European Youth Campaign – 1952-58

The rival European groups which were shepherded into the European Movement, so that they could co-operate while pursuing their own roads towards European integration, had counterparts in many youth movements which had sprung up or become reactivated after the war. These youth movements, moreover, often competed for members and their internecine rivalry deterred some of the more idealistic potential members from having anything to do with them. Perhaps because the Socialists were more conscious of the problem than others, it was André Philip, the Socialist leader, who was designated by the European Movement to form a movement which would harness these young 'militants' into working together. *La Campagne Européenne de la Jeunesse* was founded in 1951, under the auspices of the European Movement and, from the beginning, brought together traditional youth movements such as scouts and the smaller, militant political groups such as the European Federation of Young Federalists. National committees were set up in the main Western European countries and an international secretariat in Paris allocated funds and serviced the organisation.

Joseph Retinger tried to generate some interest in Ireland, as he had for the European Movement, and this time seems to have been more successful. In March 1952, he writes that he has been to Dublin, where he saw 'de Valera, Aiken, MacBride, MacEntee and Costello' (he refers to Declan, the son of the former Taoiseach, John A. Costello). 'I found everyone very favourable to our plans for the Youth Campaign in Ireland and the Government gave me its full blessing. Probably young Costello will be the leader of this Campaign in Ireland. . . .'[1]

The Irish government does not seem to have taken any steps in the matter but there were three factors which contributed to the success of the youth campaign in Ireland. The first was the fact that Declan Costello and some of those with whom he associated were interested in opening up the horizons for young people in Ireland. The second was the anxiety of those already in youth organisations to get assistance for voluntary bodies operating well, although starved of money and personnel. The third was the fact that Macra na Feirme was already aware of the European Youth Campaign through its long-standing association with the World Assembly of Youth (a largely US-financed organisation designed to support any democratic youth organisations which were prepared to affiliate. Its membership was dominated by international, non-Communist student organisations but it also had quite a number of other bodies, including '4-H Clubs' and young farmers' clubs) and anxious to expand its European contacts. Macra na Feirme not only grouped together all the young farmers' clubs in the country but was one of the most dynamic and successful organisations in the field of youth work.

It is apparent from the correspondence of this period that Retinger and others placed great reliance on the assistant to the British national secretary of the EYC, Maurice Foley.[2] Foley, of Irish extraction, had contacts with Ireland, North and South, through his involvement in the trade union movement and the Young Christian Workers and was obviously anxious to encourage the youth organisations in the Republic of Ireland to set up a national committee. The committee had its first formal meeting in January 1952 with a chairman, P. T. Hughes, from the Catholic Boy Scouts of Ireland and an honorary secretary, Geoffrey Coyle, a young barrister. It represented a very wide cross-section of voluntary organisations[3] and while some of its members may have been a bit hazy about the need for European integration they were certainly anxious to avail themselves of the opportunity to co-operate with each other and establish contacts with similar bodies outside the country.

The new body had two hurdles to overcome before it became acceptable to those in charge of youth organisations. The first arose from its very name. The word 'Campaign' was a direct translation but not a natural title in English. Allied with 'Youth' and 'European' it carried connotations of mass rallies of uniformed Communist/Fascist youngsters and was both foreign and offensive to Irish susceptibilities. And then there was the question of where the money came from. As far as Ireland was concerned, it was largely the 'American Committee on United Europe' under the presidency of General Bill Donovan and later Paul Hoffman.

The minutes of the first meeting give a good background, not only to the attitude of the Irish organisations but also to the links between the Council of Europe and the various pro-European associations in operation. Declan Costello described Dr Retinger's visit to Ireland and stressed his connection with the Council of Europe. Costello went on to describe the EYC as an offspring of the European Movement, which had been formed, 'partly as a unifying organ for the various national youth movements and partly as a counterblast to the Communist youth movement'.

All present asked for more information and by May 1952 the ad hoc committee had circulated information from Paris on the source of its funds.

> The funds of the EYC are supplied by the European Movement and they come from two sides . . . the contributions of the National Councils of the European Movement and the grants of the American Committee for United Europe, which is a completely private committee. This has never been concealed and it was clearly stated at the La Brevière meeting which was the official start of the EYC. . . . The leading body of the EYC is the governing board which functions with an equal number of members of the European Movement and of representatives of the youth organisation.

A letter from Geoffrey Coyle, sent out some time in June 1952, records his attendance at a meeting in Paris with other national secretaries of the Campaign. He speaks of the financial situation; apparently the projects submitted by the Irish youth organisations were not 'of the sort that would ordinarily receive grants but the Central Committee would very probably allocate about £500 towards these projects in order to stimulate Irish interest in the Campaign'.[4]

During these early months there are three main themes in the correspondence:

1. The EYC, as an international body, claimed that it was in a precarious financial position and could not guarantee funds for the coming year – this situation continued throughout its life. The American Committee made only annual grants.

2. While individual Irish delegates attended conferences in Florence and Edinburgh they seem to have been unable

to do much in the way of follow-up and the interest of some of the organisations seems to have declined.

3. There were some natural reservations on the part of Irish youth leaders about becoming involved in a political campaign, however democratic and laudable the objectives.

There is constant mention of a proposed visit from Robert Schuman between 1952 and the date of his death. He seems to have caught the imagination of the Irish in a manner not shared by Spaak or Adenauer. In fact he never came but both the European Movement and the EYC in Ireland spent several years waiting for Schuman.

The international secretariat of the EYC mentions Ireland in its draft programme for 1953-4. It lists the preoccupations of the Irish National Committee as: 'Distance from the European "home base" and lack of interest: few organised youth movements – few possibilities for co-ordination'.

The lack of a paid national secretary was responsible for some of the disappointments during 1952-3, so a secretary (myself) was appointed on a part-time basis in May 1954. Subsequently there was a much steadier stream of Irish delegates going abroad and European speakers coming to Ireland, plus a better follow-up to conferences and seminars. I was succeeded in 1957 by Eilish MacCurtain, but when international funds dried up in 1959 it was not possible to raise money from Irish sources to finance the secretariat and the EYC disbanded.

One of the proposals from the Irish committee was carried out in June 1954 as a European summer conference in Dun Laoghaire, County Dublin. This five-day conference was an impressive mixture of culture, education and recreation. Dr Donal O'Sullivan, the chairman of the Irish Council of the European Movement, charted the history of 'the European idea' (the usual subject with which conferences in Ireland were started); Professor Daniel Villey (Professor of Laws, University of Poitiers) dealt with 'European Political Problems', particularly those relating to political unity and defence; Maurice Foley, the British secretary of the EYC, spoke on 'Youth Problems' and other speakers discussed economics, communications and related subjects. The main point of interest for the purpose of this study is the result of the group discussions which took place during the conference and were presented on the final day. The group dealing with 'political problems' laid great stress on Britain's position (which reflected the interest of all the delegates and particularly those attending from Northern Ireland). After mentioning Britain's defence commitments in Europe and the European Defence Community, the rapporteur goes on: 'Great Britain's reluctance to join Europe is mainly psychological, a dislike of European institutions and a sense of confidence in their own'. Attention was paid to France, Germany, Scandinavia, the EDC, economic changes and a comparison was made of the 'functional approach in OEEC and EPU and federal in ECSC'. Nothing specific is said of the Republic of Ireland but the tone and content of the conference must have given the Irish delegates a European understanding and vocabulary, which they would not have easily found elsewhere at that time.

One important aspect of the EYC's work in Ireland which only appears incidentally from the files but which has been commented on by most of those who were involved at that time was the co-operation which existed between the Campaign in Dublin and in Belfast. Northern Ireland came under London but had a regional committee and secretary, as had Scotland and Wales. The Northern Ireland secretary was Stratton Mills who, as a Young Unionist, was acceptable to the majority in the North but who also had on his committee several Young Christian Workers who, as Catholics and trade unionists, represented quite a different strand of politics.

E. G. Thompson, who handled a lot of the English-language meetings for the international secretariat of the EYC, attended some of the conferences in Ireland and speaks enthusiastically about the pioneer work done by the two committees. He felt at the time there was a real possibility for co-operation within the framework of a European Community and that even the guarded discussions which took place at 'work-shops' during the conferences were a break-through for both sides.

EYC activities increased in 1955, both North and South of the Border, and in March 1956 the Dublin committee was able to launch an occasional publication, *Commentary*, to publicise its work and carry reports of conferences attended abroad by Irish delegates. This proved useful, not only to maintain continuity but also as a record.

The most ambitious undertaking of the EYC was probably an international student conference held in University College, Galway from 17-21 May 1956, on 'The Social Implications of a United Europe' attended by several hundred students, addressed by Éamon de Valera, Seán MacBride, Liam Cosgrave, the Minister for External Affairs, and well reported in the national press. There were various foreign speakers, notably M. Lucien de Groote of the International Movement of Christian Democrats and the workshops covered a most ambitious programme.

Did the European Youth Campaign do any more than publicise what was happening in Europe and encourage its Irish members to play some part in European activities? Certainly, there were no resolutions, no *revendications* and no torch-light processions in favour of a united Europe as were organised in Strasbourg and elsewhere on occasion. Most of the literature used at the Irish meetings was translated from the French (as relatively little of the British material was regarded as entirely suitable – preoccupied as the British were with the Commonwealth, the implications of NATO and Europe and a rather different scale and historical association with Europe). The Irish literature, therefore, leaned rather heavily on the side of the federalist idea of unification. This was hardly surprising when it is recalled that Hendrik Brugmans and André Philip played such important roles in the EYC.

A pamphlet used in Ireland at that time contains strong Federal meat, calling for a regrouping of the traditional political parties and lightly mentioning the differences which exist between 'Europeans' and the autonomists and the federalists.[5]

The use of such material required considerable explanation on the part of the organisers, usually the national secretary, but the national committee itself did not take a specific stand on the different approaches to European integration which were advocated. Its composition, with a preponderance of strictly non-political youth organisations, made it impossible to become involved with any ideological movement and while 'co-operation' was an acceptable term, 'federalism' was a controversial one.

The Universities

All good universities are open to the outside world and there were, therefore, traditional European links with the Irish universities, but the isolation imposed by the war years had had an effect on academic life. Immediately after the war, however, there was an influx of mature British students to Trinity College to take up studies previously prevented by military service and this added to the 'English' flavour of the university. The three Colleges of the National University also benefitted from the inclusion of a considerable number of non-Irish students during the same period. Cork, in particular, had a substantial group of Polish and East European students and University College, Dublin and Trinity College both had quite a number of Irish-American ex-servicemen studying on GI grants. The medical and law faculties also received students from Africa and Asia. This mixture of nationalities, plus the higher average age of the foreign students, had a marked and, on the whole, leavening effect on the native Irish undergraduates.

It is notoriously difficult to ascertain the numbers involved in student societies; records are patchy at best and often lost or destroyed by succeeding generations. It would appear, however, from the recollections of some of those most involved in student activities in the late forties and early fifties that there was quite a vigorous extracurricular life available for the minority who wanted it and that many of the societies provided an introduction to European cultural and social life to students whose secondary school horizons had been very limited. Allowing for the retrospective glow that usually suffuses such reminiscences, it would seem that student societies involved with drama, debating and economics were anxious to keep abreast of developments on the mainland of Europe. The history and various language societies were particularly aware of Ireland's 'European' dimension and if the students had to rely rather heavily on theoretical discussions and contacts with the small number of non-Irish on the university staff at that time it was because of lack of funds rather than lack of initiative.

It would be unwise to regard the Irish universities as stimulating, challenging academies of wisdom and vision without taking into account the imperfections and constraints which many students found frustrating and discouraging. Too many part-time professors, occasional mediocrities, a certain inbred pattern of recruitment in some faculties, undoubtedly affected the influence wielded by the universities, particularly on students who attended only because of parental decisions or the need to get a professional qualification. With hindsight, however, the positive contribution made by Irish academics during the forties and fifties must be judged in the context of a population, North and South, of four and a quarter million people who had been effectively isolated from the mainland of Europe for a very long time.

Student organisations

There are three student organisations named as members of the National Council of the EYC. The *Irish Association of Catholic University Students* was a federation of Catholic student societies in Queen's University, Belfast and the University Colleges of Cork, Dublin and Galway. It was affiliated to Pax Romana, the international movement of Catholic students, founded in 1921 and at this period enjoying a revival in Europe and elsewhere.

Its first Congress, held in University College, Galway in 1951, was on 'The Catholic University Student' and the implications for Irish students of what this could mean for their co-religionists in Eastern Europe, Latin America, Asia and Africa. The following year the Congress went to

Queen's in Belfast and in 1953 the Cork Congress was on the subject of 'Catholics and European Unity'. The Congresses lasted for about a week and were attended by about two hundred students each year. That for 1956, held again in Queen's, on 'Spotlight on Catholicism – The Ideal and Reality in Ireland' included lectures on 'Catholicism in Public Life' by Dr Alfred O'Rahilly and 'Ireland in International Affairs' by Liam Cosgrave, the Minister for External Affairs, and 'The Church in Eastern Europe' by Dr Stanislaus Grocholski, a former Polish diplomat and Chairman of the Federation of Poles in Great Britain.

IACUS had its vicissitudes during its existence (1947-63) and there is an agenda of a council meeting, called in 1960 with an item: 'The future of IACUS – to continue or be disbanded?' but it fulfilled a need for a challenge in thought and action at a time when Irish students needed outside stimulus. Because of its papal approval and impeccable credentials it was able to discuss matters of controversy in a manner which would have aroused instant disapproval from university and ecclesiastical authorities if done under a secular banner.

The *Irish Students Association* was the official representative body for university students and acted as an umbrella organisation. Its membership of the EYC was useful insofar as it enabled some ISA officers to attend meetings abroad on occasion and provided a link with student societies when a conference of European interest was being held in Ireland. It had little contact however with the general body of students.

Dublin University Association for International Affairs was the third student body listed as involved in the EYC. As the name indicates this was a society in Trinity College; it was founded just after the war and flourished under the wing of Dr Donal O'Sullivan, who had been given a post in International Affairs under the aegis of the Department of History. It was cultivated by some of the non-Irish students, particularly those of Polish origin, and is mentioned separately here because it was an individual member of the European Youth Campaign and obviously saw itself as having a wider role than that of the traditional College society.

The Dublin University Association for International Affairs provided delegates for conferences both at home and abroad on aspects of European integration and pre-dated the interest shown by older bodies such as the Hist (the College Historical Society) and the Law Society which naturally became involved through debates and inaugural meetings in the Free Trade versus Common Market controversy in the second half of the fifties.

The EYC also included organisations such as the Boy Scouts of Ireland, the Catholic Boy Scouts of Ireland, Comhairle le Leas Oige and the Girl Guides, which provided individuals who were prepared to become involved; indeed, the chairman of the national committee, P. T. Hughes, was a senior member of the Catholic Boy Scouts of Ireland. The ordinary members of these organisations, however, were not really touched by its activities. An occasional youth seminar at home would be supported and one or two members would be selected to attend a relevant conference in The Netherlands, France or the United Kingdom but that was the extent of the contact.

The Irish Countrywomen's Association was another member organisation which used the EYC to provide speakers for its guilds throughout the country and to send some of its young members to meetings in Europe which were of interest. Indeed, during this period the ICA successfully used Foras Éireann, the Kellogg Foundation and the lesser facilities provided by the EYC to build up its educational activities prior to the establishment of a residential college in Termonfeckin as a centre of adult education.

The Irish Council of the European Movement

The first attempts to form an Irish Council of the European Movement took place immediately after the European Congress of The Hague in 1948. They failed because Seán MacBride, who was very interested, would not, as Minister for External Affairs, form such a national committee and because Senator Douglas was prepared to support but not to organise or preside over such a body. Professor Michael Tierney was not particularly enthusiastic and Senator Eleanor Butler, the third Irish delegate to the Congress, was heavily committed to work on the local government level. Yet the initial prospects had looked good.

Senator Douglas moved a motion in the Seanad, after his return from The Congress of The Hague, 'That Seanad Éireann directs the attention of the Government to the resolutions in favour of a United Europe which were passed at the Congress of Europe at The Hague and requests the Minister for External Affairs to make a statement'.[6] (The Minister, Seán MacBride, was in attendance.) In his speech Senator Douglas made specific mention of his intention to draw the attention of the public to the 'movement towards European unity which is gaining support amongst members of all political parties in Western Europe except the Communists'. He claimed that there had been a growth of interest in European Affairs in Ireland since the end of the war. He asked what he considered the vital questions: 'Can peace be maintained in a divided Europe? Can any European nation stand alone against the dangers (which threaten)? Can a divided Europe maintain principles of democracy and individual freedom?' Advocates of European unity believed the answers to be in the negative.

Having described the Congress of Europe of The Hague 7-10 May 1948 he mentioned the Irish delegation and read and discussed the political and economic resolutions. Referring to the former he dwelt on the reference to the creation of a European Political Assembly. 'Without some surrender of sovereignty no real federation is possible.' He personally favoured the creation of a European Assembly provided that it did not attempt to do too much. People who attempt too much are the 'worst enemies' of the united Europe. 'I believe that a healthy and honest nationalism is as necessary to internationalism as a high standard of individual character is essential to a good society.' He also mentions the difficulties facing representatives of small countries in the European Assembly.

As regards the economic resolution Douglas supported the objectives but was concerned about the proposed means to achieve them. '. . . while I am in sympathy with the ideal of the resolution I am sceptical of the proposal for a full customs union as an ultimate objective'. Referring to the cultural resolution, Senator Douglas emphasised the importance of indigenous national culture and the idea that unity and uniformity are not synonymous. He called for the greatest possible cultural interchange between Ireland and the rest of Europe.

The proposal was seconded by Eleanor Butler, who specifically mentioned the inadequate newspaper reports of the Congress and feared that the public had no idea of the extent of the discussions nor the measure of agreement reached by so many disparate groups.

> Surely, we as a nation are capable of seeing the wider issues of providing the world with a new ideology, even of seeing the benefits which it might bring to our own country, even of seeing the possibility of the constitutional position – that unreal position which we all resent so much, our own particular grievance – collapse like a pack of cards. The resolutions for a united Europe, which would include the abolition of Customs barriers and European passports, I feel would even abolish the artificial border. If that were done, what is left? It even eliminates the necessity of having to make up our minds whether we are or are not in the Commonwealth, and whether we go in or stay out. With all this out of the way, what is left? Surely, then, our own grievance and our own particular question should not be made a bargaining issue. Surely, our people can at least be given an opportunity to play their part in European and international peace and security and in resisting any policy of aggression.

There was no follow-up to these two speeches but the reports from Retinger remained unfailingly optimistic. In August 1948 he reports a meeting in University College, Dublin, as guest of Professor Tierney, attended by a group of 'influential' people, as a result of which a provisional committee was elected. Nothing further is heard of this committee but in November 1949 Senator Douglas reports the formation of an 'Irish Parliamentary Group' and indicates that it would like to attend meetings in 1950 – finances permitting.

It was only after the formation of the European Youth Campaign in Ireland that another serious effort was made to set up the adult body and this time it was launched under the wing of an academic, Dr Donal O'Sullivan, lecturer in International Affairs in TCD, former Clerk of the Senate, authority on early Irish music (on which he worked in University College, Dublin) and well-known author and lecturer. There were many small meetings during the second half of 1953 and eventually a public meeting was held in the Shelbourne Hotel, Dublin in January 1954 to elect a committee and launch an Irish Council of the European Movement. Donal O'Sullivan was elected chairman; General Liam Archer, vice-chairman; Brendan Malin (of the Irish News Agency), honorary secretary; Geoffrey Coyle, honorary treasurer; and Seán MacBride, Brian O'Connor and Michael Yeats, members of the executive committee. Membership was later fixed at £1 per annum and seven shillings and sixpence for those under twenty-five years of age.

Most of the functions seem to have taken a long time to organise and the tendency to hold all meetings of the executive at very short notice did not encourage a very high attendance. With the exception of a few lectures given by people like Salvador de Madariaga and General Anders there was little obvious activity and even the servicing of the Council by the European Youth Campaign office only improved the position marginally.

In 1959 Garret FitzGerald and some of the economists who had become involved in European affairs decided to relaunch a revamped Irish Council of the European Movement. Dr Donal O'Sullivan was elected president, Garret FitzGerald became chairman, Denis Corboy was appointed secretary and Seán Lemass, as Minister for Industry and Commerce, and later Taoiseach, became actively associated with the movement.

The reason behind the new interest and change in focus is evident from a memorandum sent to all members prior to an annual general meeting called for 6 March 1959. After a brief introductory paragraph (in which it is said that 'The emphasis varies in different countries and in Ireland there has never been any political objective'), the document goes on to state:

> The coming of the European Economic Community and the possibility of setting up a European Free Trade Area has led the European Movemènt in several countries to focus its activities on economic problems. It is emphasised that the Irish Council has no bias one way or the other and regards itself purely as a fact finding organisation. Thus its primary function is to gather, collate and digest information in European Economic Affairs from all sources. One of our principal sources of information will be of course our corresponding Councils in other countries whose offices have been working on these problems for some years. It will be the object of the Irish Council to disseminate this information among the interested parties here. . . .
>
> In endeavouring to carry out its fundamental objectives the Irish Council has the approval and support of the Minister for Industry and Commerce.

This marks a change of emphasis for the Irish Council but was apparently accepted by the veterans of the Movement who were pleased enough to try the new approach in return for the backing of political and business interests which had hitherto ignored them. Some left, but others, like Donal O'Sullivan himself, stayed on even though their influence was no longer very strong. By the autumn the new programme was well under way as were plans for a newsletter and the publication of a pamphlet. Group membership had been introduced and the Council was obviously on a firmer financial footing.

The European Economic conference organised in Dublin by the Irish Council (20 July 1959) on 'Recent Economic Developments in Europe' was built round the speeches of four visiting speakers: Walter Hallstein, President of the

European Commission, Alfred Robens, former Minister of Labour in the UK, Maurice Faure, former French Foreign Secretary and J. Flint Cahan, Deputy Secretary-General of OEEC and attracted considerable attention and support for the Movement.[7] A commentator in 'The Irish Review and Annual 1959' (which could have been written by Garret FitzGerald himself), having stated that the Irish government had not been sufficiently well-informed about the implications of the current economic developments in Europe, went on to deal extensively with the Conference.

> Whatever part he played in it, there is no doubt that before Mr. John Cahan, the Deputy Secretary-General of OEEC, spoke in Dublin in July, the Government had been dragging its feet, and, after he spoke, went into action. . . . Referring to the outline Outer Seven agreement which was being prepared, he said: 'I think you badly needed a jolt. Some of you were getting a bit complacent. . . . You are now going to lose, probably forever, your privileged position in the UK agricultural market.'
>
> There was a strong reaction among some higher civil servants and even Ministers against Mr Cahan's speech, which probably was deliberately exaggerated. But it had its effect. In August the dim beginnings of a plan formed in the Government's mind. In the first place, application was made to the Common Market Commission in Brussels for the opening of diplomatic relations with the Commission. Secondly, requests were sent to all the members of both Six and Seven to extend to Ireland temporarily and unilaterally all the tariff and quota concessions they were giving one another.
>
> Thirdly, an Anglo-Irish Trade Committee was established. It met first in September, but its progress was held up by the British election.[8]

There was widespread discussion on Ireland and the Free Trade Area and on Ireland and the Common Market from 1958 onwards. *The Leader* editorialised: 'It has been said that the time lag for European ideas to reach Ireland is nearly a quarter of a century. This time we had better cut it short for our whole economic way of life may be at stake. The United States of Europe is arising and we are outside it . . .'[9] and the same paper in a later issue congratulated Dr Donal O'Sullivan and Garret FitzGerald for organising the Economic Conference mentioned above.[10]

Not all those interested in Irish involvement in European affairs were, however, equally enthusiastic about the new direction the debate was taking. Lt General Michael J. Costello (Chief Executive of Comhlucht Siúicre Éireann) is quoted as expressing grave reservations at the overemphasis on trade and he emphasised the political implications and obligations which were spelled out in the Treaty of Rome and were implicit in any close form of association acceptable to the rest of Western Europe.[11] General Costello on several occasions crossed swords with Garret FitzGerald on what he considered to be a lack of frankness in informing the Irish public of the inevitable consequences of free trade associations which might become open to them. The academics, too, began to drift away and the creation of the European Teachers Association within a few years involved some of them again on a more cultural and educational level.

In 1960 the Irish Council of the European Movement was invited to set up an Irish section of the European League for Economic Co-operation which had been founded in 1946 by groups of politicians, trade unionists, economists and businessmen, with headquarters in Brussels. It was one of the movements which organised the Congress of The Hague in 1948. Seán MacBride had had contacts with ELEC in the late forties, mainly through his friendship with Van Zeeland, the former Foreign Minister of Belgium and the first president of the organisation. It had never taken root in Ireland, however, partly because there was no internal pressure from the banking or business world to have it, and partly because the absence of Ireland from both the EFTA and the EEC resulted in no requests from the other members to set up a branch in an isolated country.

At the time when the issue of membership of the European Community was very much alive, it is interesting to note the composition of the Executive elected at the AGM of the Irish Council of the European Movement on 2 February 1961. Dr Donal O'Sullivan was elected president, unopposed. The members of the executive were: Lt Col. J. E. Armstrong (Irish Whiskey Distillers' Assoc.), Dr C. A. Cusack (Clondalkin Paper Mills), Dr Juan J. Greene (National Farmers' Assoc.), Mr R. W. S. Greene (Arthur Guinness Son & Co.), Mr Sean Healy (NFA), Mr A. J. Kehoe (W. & H. M. Goulding Ltd.), Mr Fintan Kennedy (Irish Transport & General Workers' Union), Mr Michael O'Reilly (Irish Whiskey Distillers Assoc.), Dr Louis Smith (NFA), Mr E. F. Sutton (Goodbody Ltd.), and as individuals – Mr Denis Corboy, Mr Garret FitzGerald, Dr J. I. FitzPatrick, Mr Seán MacBride SC, and Mr J. C. Tonge. Garret FitzGerald was subsequently elected chairman at the first Executive Meeting.

The minutes of the meetings show that there were many contacts with Brussels, London and other European centres and occasional Irish meetings outside Dublin. One entry in the minutes of the meeting of 10 July 1961 indicates the concern taken over Lemass's attitude to entry to the EEC. 'A lengthy discussion ensued about as to how we should make our views known to the Government, and it was finally decided that verbal approach by the Chairman to An Taoiseach before July 18th (the date of An Taoiseach's visit to London) would be best.'

The Irish Council of the European Movement suffered the vicissitudes of any voluntary organisation in the succeeding years. It was always rather short of money and occasionally of manpower. It was artificially strengthened to fight a campaign for joining the EEC prior to the referendum on that issue in 1973 and it received a special grant of £10,000 from the Department of External Affairs in 1971. The interest taken in it by the political parties and business world after Garret FitzGerald reconstituted it in 1959 and Seán Lemass took an active interest in its proceedings ensured its survival – even after the proposal to join had been won and the fever abated. Its greatest strength has been that it represented a cross-section of Irish social, political and sectional interests and that it was able to maintain internal harmony in its efforts to involve Ireland in the community of Europe. The admission of members of the Labour Party and some prominent trade unionists, albeit in a personal capacity, to the Executive of the Council after Ireland's admission to the EEC redressed the imbalance which had been created by their absence in the years under review.

The Rural Organisations

The record of initiative, organisational ability and awareness of international developments shown by the farming community in Ireland between 1948 and 1960, in both long-established and new organisations, is impressive. Set against the economic and political background of the period it is outstanding.

Given the preponderance of agriculture in the Irish economy, particularly in the early years of the state, it is not surprising that there was often talk about forming a 'farmers' party'. Such parties were common enough on the European mainland, but the fusion of the land and independence issues into the broad movement of nationalism in Ireland and the lack of a significant industrial arm in the economy (against which agriculture might feel impelled to organise) militated against such a party becoming a major political force.

A Farmers' Party was represented in Dáil Éireann between 1922 and 1932 and was largely conservative in outlook and derived support from the larger and more prosperous farmers. Professor F. S. L. Lyons notes that 'a handful of its surviving members were attracted to the short-lived National Centre Party in the early thirties, but thereafter the wealthier members of the farming community tended to identify with Fine Gael.'[1]

There were, however, several attempts to harness the small farmers' vote, the most serious of which resulted in the formation of Clann na Talmhan, in Galway in 1938. The party drew most of its support from small and medium-sized farmers and their families and was strongest in the west of Ireland. It was led by Michael Donnellan and reached its zenith when it won ten seats in the General Election in 1943.

The divisions caused by the civil war, the conflict of interests seen between the small-holders and big farmers and the tendency of small political parties to fragment and wither away explain why the rural organisations, Macra na Feirme, the National Farmers Association and the Irish Countrywomen's Association in particular, refused to allow their movements to be transformed into political parties or even to permit members of their executive to be candidates in local or general elections.

Macra na Feirme

Macra na Feirme (which was founded in 1944) had three unusual characteristics in the first ten years of its existence. The first was its liberal interpretation of the term 'young' (indeed, one advantage of the Irish title was that it implied no age limitation, being roughly translated as 'sons of farmers' rather than Young Farmers). The second was its close relationship with a group of specialists and academics in economics, agriculture and related sciences whose expert advice was frequently sought and freely given to the new association and its various committees. Not only was there no 'anti-intellectual' bias but it is quite clear from the speakers and writers used by Macra that they looked for the best brains available in the country and used them. Thirdly, it is clear that the leaders were conscious of events happening outside Ireland and anxious to let all their members know about them and how they might affect Ireland. From Macra's international connections it soon became clear that the problems of Irish farming were nearer to those of Western Europe than to the US and that the creation of a 'Green Pool' in Europe (i.e., the first attempt to form a common agricultural market in the fifties) was worth investigating seriously. At this time (the early fifties) no political party, government department, trade union or professional organisation in Ireland was publicly discussing the possible repercussions of a strong European Community on their own country but the matter came up even as a question of debate in club competitions run by Macra na Feirme.

Looking back on this period it is also remarkable how the organisation welded together the 'strong' and small farmers of the time. Not all were enamoured of the new growth and it was not equally strong throughout the country but it represented a common bond between farmers who had not previously considered that their interests were compatible. In its first ten years of existence, Macra na Feirme tended to represent the ambitious and progressive farmer, whether big or small, cattle or milk producer, mixed farmer or 'rancher'. Lest it be thought that the educational activities were purely altruistic it is useful to quote Seán Healy, who, as secretary of Macra na Feirme had gone on to become the first general secretary of the National Farmers' Association in 1955. When asked why he considered the international activities of the NFA so important Healy replied:

> I think that it is terribly important, and always thought that it was terribly important, because from the time that I joined Macra na Feirme in 1948, it was obvious that we were no longer working in the context of agricultural products for our own requirements. We were now on the export market. . . . We had been in the young farmers in Macra na Feirme associated with the European Youth Campaign and with the World Assembly of Youth. In the NFA, when it was established, we joined the International Federation of Agricultural Producers and, before the Government applied for membership of the EEC we advocated membership of the EEC . . . It has been shown in the past few years that through our association with other countries and through these contacts, that our negotiations will ensure that the Irish viewpoint is heard in the World forum and particularly at this stage in the EEC forum.[2]

The difficulties of catering for a very wide disparity in ages led to the formation of Macra na Tuaithe in 1952. This was definitely a junior branch of Macra na Feirme and designed for those between twelve and eighteen. It had debates and discussions like the parent body, but on a junior level. Macra na Tuaithe was also a member of the European Youth Campaign but the records of that organisation show that it was mainly the organisers who attended conferences on European affairs in Ireland and abroad.

The Farming Unions

It was obvious that the various commodity sub-committees set up by Macra na Feirme, plus the Beet Growers Association and the Liquid Milk Group, would eventually want to exercise pressure on both the market and the government independently of an educational and voluntary body such as Macra na Feirme. The first overt move was the foundation of the Irish Creamery Milk Suppliers' Association in Limerick in 1950, set up to cater for farmers engaged in intensive dairy farming and therefore stronger in the Golden Vale (i.e., Limerick, Tipperary and parts of Cork and Kerry). In February 1953, the ICMSA carried out the first widespread milk strike in Ireland. It lasted for sixteen days and caused considerable resentment in the urban sector of the population but it wrested an increase of 1¾d per gallon for milk from the government of the day and it served notice that the farming community was prepared to use methods previously thought to be the sole weapon of the trade unions.

There were clashes of personality and policy between the ICMSA and the National Farmers Association, when that body was later formed in 1955, and the ICMSA does not feature as prominently as other farming groups in discussions on European affairs in the fifties. The Irish Creamery Milk Suppliers' Association, however, came from the same stable as the NFA and its publications show that it, too, was concerned about European and international developments, at least insofar as they affected its main commodity, milk.

Since there are few records of the early years of Macra na Feirme extant, the involvement of the organisation in European activities has to be reconstructed through the documentary fragments of other bodies, notably the European Youth Campaign. The national secretary of Macra, Seán Healy, was a member of the EYC from its formation and had been associated with the European Committee of WAY. Speakers were brought from Denmark and Holland from the earliest days and used for Macra clubs in Kildare, Wicklow, Louth, Mayo and throughout the country. There was quite an ambitious meeting in Athy in 1953 at which Per Federspel, chairman of the Agricultural Committee of the Council of Europe, spoke on the possibility of a 'Green Pool' for European farmers' produce.

By January 1956 the two-way traffic of speakers and representatives between Ireland and the European Community countries is much more firmly established and Macra na Feirme and the National Farmers Association combine with the EYC to organise, for example, a series of lectures by Dr J. J. van der Lee, Director of International Organisations in the Netherlands Ministry for Agriculture, Fisheries and Food on the current developments in Europe. Dr van der Lee spoke in Wexford and Dublin and his biggest meeting was in Balbriggan. A special series of courses on European topics in the Agricultural University of Wageningen in the Netherlands was attended by an average of two Irish delegates per session. Since an address by Dr Siccho Mansholt was usually the highlight of these gatherings it is not surprising to find Irish rural leaders well aware of what was happening in the growing European Economic Community. Nor is it strange to find Macra na Feirme debating 'Free Trade versus the Treaty of Rome' (at a public speaking competition in Kildare, November 1956) and coming down fairly heavily on the side of the Six, without, be it admitted, any too clear idea as yet where Ireland might find a place in the European Community.

The success, from the farmers' viewpoint, of the ICMSA strengthened the move towards a national farmers' union which would include all farmers and all commodities. It would have come very quickly indeed were it not for two important points on which the different leaders could not agree. The first was the need to make a farmers' union strictly non-political in the party sense, to the extent of excluding members of the Oireachtas from holding office in its executive. Macra na Feirme and the ICMSA were adamant on this point while the Beetgrowers' Association insisted that practising politicians should not be disbarred in this way. The second difference of opinion arose between the ICMSA and Macra na Feirme and concerned the method of reaching decisions. The ICMSA envisaged a federal type organisation which would refer back major policy decisions to each constituent organisation while Macra na Feirme considered such a body too cumbersome. Eventually, the National Farmers Association was formed in January 1955 and soon became the most influential voice of farmers in the country.

It is significant that the guest speakers to the inaugural meeting in Dublin included Arthur Algeo, the then President of the Ulster Farmers Union, Lt Gen. M. J. Costello, William Howard Taft III, US ambassador to Ireland, the president of the National Farmers Union of Britain and the president of the Belgian Farmers Union. Within three months close links were established with the Ulster Farmers Union and the good relationship then established lasted through the succeeding decades. Almost immediately, too, the NFA became members of the European Committee of FIAP and the CEA.[3] It took its international commitments seriously and frequently provided chairmen and rapporteurs for committees dealing with beef, dairying, grain, pigs and bacon, sugar beet, poultry and every aspect of agricultural production carried out in Ireland.[4] The Irish farmers were regarded with respect, partly because they were obviously well organised and well briefed and also because they carried considerable political weight in their home country (a point not always acknowledged by the farmers themselves).

Muintir na Tíre

It is difficult to classify Muintir na Tíre. Its genesis was the foundation of a co-operative, Muintir na Tíre Ltd, by a Tipperary curate, Father M J Hayes in 1931. It was restructured in 1937 and set up a system of Guilds, based on the parish boundary, with special sections for farmers, labourers, business and professional men, women and youth, and objectives which were both social and economic.[5] Great stress was laid on the need for a parish meeting-place and parish halls were soon dotted around the countryside wherever a Muintir guild had established itself.

Father Hayes was well aware of the post-war efforts to unite Europe and sympathetic to much of their philosophy. The support of Pope Pius XII[6] would have guaranteed a favourable hearing in any case and the fact that the Christian Democrat parties in Italy, France and Germany advocated integration was an added attraction. This is not to say that Muintir na Tíre was looking for close political union with the Six – or with anybody else – in the late forties and early fifties, but it was open to consideration of the idea and frequently used European-minded speakers for its various discussions and gatherings. The examples of the Catholic parties and rural organisations in Belgium and The Netherlands in their work for the social and economic development of the depressed rural areas in their respective countries were frequently cited, and though the organisation never envisaged itself becoming a political party it was conscious of the political power which a strong, socially oriented organisation based in the villages and towns of Ireland could wield.

After the death of Canon (as he had become) Hayes in 1957, Muintir na Tíre naturally changed character and after the inevitable difficulties of readjustment became even more a social and economic rather than agricultural organisation. It seized the opportunity afforded by the debate on entry into the European Community to stress its own role as watchdog of social development outside the main centres of population and industry and has maintained this since entry into the EEC.

The Co-operative Movement

The Irish co-operative movement has been successful largely – almost exclusively – in the agricultural field; except for the Belfast Co-operative Society which is closer to many of the big British concerns, there was no production co-operative in the cities and towns.

The movement, directed by the Irish Agricultural Organisation Society Ltd, was in difficulties during the forties and fifties and a far-reaching report was commissioned.[7] Because, however, of its emphasis on creameries and milk supplies IAOS does not feature in the same manner as did the other organisations already mentioned and where its members were actively interested – as many of them were – they usually made their views known on the platform of other rural organisations. It is perhaps significant that, in his four-hundred page history, Patrick Bolger has only two references to the European Communities. In one, he mentions that the representatives of the Federation of Irish Fishing Co-operatives (founded in 1968) 'played a prominent part in the negotiations preceding Ireland's entry into the European Community' and in the other he complains that, 'there is as yet no full commitment on the part of the societies about the future role and structures of the IAOS. Accession to the European Community has put additional strain both on the finances and the manhours of the organisation society, and progress is meantime halted whilst the co-ops withhold money and fail to agree on structural details'.[8]

* * *

The importance of agriculture and the rural organisations both to domestic developments and European involvement during the period under review cannot be overemphasised. When Ireland first sent its representatives to Paris in July 1947 to discuss the European Recovery Programme, the manner in which the country could best contribute to reconstruction was summed up in the first paragraph of the study of the Irish economy prepared by international experts.[9]

> Ireland's principal problem is the restoration of agricultural production and Ireland's main contribution to European recovery will take place through the produc-

> tion of more food for export. Since the economy of Ireland is closely related to that of the United Kingdom the major part of increased food exports will probably go there. To expand its exports of agricultural products, Ireland needs to mechanize its agriculture, obtain more fertilisers and animal feedstuffs, increase its imports of fuel and overhaul its transportation system.

In the 1950s the export market for Irish agriculture was still very largely confined to the United Kingdom. But the encouragement of British agriculture closed outlets for commodities such as eggs which had been taken for granted in 1938. The British need to encourage good relations with the other members of EFTA led to the regulation of imports by quota (this was particularly marked for butter and bacon in the early sixties). Thus the special relationship between the two countries was gradually disappearing. The Irish exporter, both farmer and industrialist, was being squeezed between EFTA countries and the farmers of the United Kingdom.

This squeeze seriously reduced any choice which the Irish producers or their government might have had as to where and how the farmers would sell their produce.

> Foreign markets could no longer be taken for granted. The heirs of the 1920s rejoiced to see their values had been adopted. In the years after 1958 they were to learn that conditions abroad had changed in the thirty years and that their policies, however admirable intellectually, were no longer relevant to contemporary conditions.[10]

In these circumstances it is not surprising that farmers should have regarded the negotiations in the late fifties with more than academic interest, nor that they should have mounted pressure on politicians, public opinion, and the civil service to end the oppressive dependence on the British market. The positive involvement of the farming community, whether individually or through their organisations, in all the debates about Ireland's relationship with the new political and economic grouping in Western

Europe, is noticeable throughout the period under review and when no debate existed they started one.[11]

Outside the Debate

The formal presentation of a series of events and the attempt to show the effects they had on the life and attitude of those whom they touched lead, inevitably, to an over-tidy view of the period. There were several very important sectors of Irish life which did not publicly react to or even seem to take part in the discussion on European integration. The most obvious is, perhaps, the hierarchy of the Roman Catholic Church whose members were probably better aware than most of events in Europe through their official and personal contacts. The Catholic Archbishop of Dublin, Most Rev. Dr John Charles McQuaid, was even asked by Joseph Retinger to assume the presidency of the Irish Council of the European Movement and declined. Although Dr McQuaid was both well informed about and privately sympathetic to Irish involvement in efforts to unite Europe he did not publicly pronounce on this or any other aspect of European unity, nor did any of his colleagues. At a later stage, not covered by this study, the Rev. Dr Ian Paisley of Northern Ireland was to denounce violently the Rome Treaty and all it stood for but otherwise there seems to be no contemporary record of any public statements by prominent churchmen on the matters under review.

The Trade Unions

The heated debate on whether a European Community would be a giant cartel, a hammer with which capitalism would strike its most decisive blow against the workers or become a bulwark against the big multinationals which would give a protection manifestly beyond the power of national states, which raged in continental Europe during the fifties, never affected Ireland. The repercussions of the Cold War were felt, as were the bitter disputes about peace and international solidarity which split the international trade union movement. But the blueprint set out in the Treaty of the European Coal and Steel Community and the proposals for a European Economic Community raised no ripple whatsoever in Irish trade union waters. Individual Irish delegates to international meetings were often challenged by their European colleagues but they remained convinced that the Irish situation was unique, incapable of analysis by European outsiders and that the European experiments were, in any event, irrelevant to Irish conditions.

The Irish trade union movement was certainly in a difficult situation. Historically, it was an offshoot of the British trade union movement and its structure resembled the British one. Furthermore, the leaders had been trained in Britain, and they shared a deep-rooted distrust of French and German and Italian workers' movements, reinforced by the events of the thirties. The English language was another common bond. Yet Ireland was not a mirror image of Britain. It was primarily an agricultural country trying to industrialise in a hurry. More importantly, in the trade union context, it was a politically divided country and the trade union movement, which predated the political division, had to operate under two distinct and mutually hostile regimes.

The most intractable problem of the Irish trade union movement, however, was a deep divergence in outlook on the true role of the trade union movement as a whole. After smouldering for a long time this erupted in a split in the movement in 1945, as a result of which there were two Irish Congresses of trade unions: *The Irish Trade Union Congress,* composed of the Workers' Union of Ireland, led by James Larkin, plus the amalgamated' or British-based unions and *The Congress of Irish Unions,* composed of the big Irish Transport and General Workers' Union, led by William O'Brien, plus some small, Irish-based unions.[1]

There was a clash of personalities between Jim Larkin and William O'Brien but this was not the main reason for the split. William O'Brien retired in 1946 and Big Jim' died in early 1947, but the split was not healed until 1959. The division was between those who, like Larkin, believed that workers should strive for the break-up of the capitalist society and those, like O'Brien and Foran, who felt that the needs of the nation should be reflected in the trade union movement and the unions should work for the betterment of their members, while leaving these free to follow whatever political philosophy they preferred. It was the immemorial difference among socialists between revolution and reformism.'[2] When reconciliation was finally effected it is significant that Jack MacGougan, the prominent Northern leader and president of the ITUC, welcomed the draft constitution of the Congress as a landmark in the evolution of trade union structures in this country (because) it seeks to provide the basis of unity between two different conceptions of trade union organisation'.[3]

The energies of the trade union leadership were therefore fairly fully occupied, apart altogether from the fact that they were trying to cope with new and controversial legislation, particularly from Dublin, and to overcome the worst effects of very severe economic conditions. Any attempt to raise the issue of membership of the European Community would have been as welcome to delegates at national conferences as an invitation to discuss indulgences at an ecumenical congress.

Affiliation to the different international trade union movements was also affected by the national division. The Irish Trade Union Congress had been a member of the World Federation of Trade Unions since its establishment in Paris in 1945 but when the WFTU broke apart under the strain of the Cold War the ITUC sought affiliation with the International Confederation of Free Trade Unions, while the Congress of Irish Unions later established links with the International Federation of Christian Trade Unions. Delegates were sent to conferences abroad and some contacts were kept but both Irish congresses found the affiliation fees too high and never pursued membership more actively.

The absence of Irish trade unions from the various movements involved in promoting or at least discussing Ireland's place in a united Europe was not very serious in the early years. Had the leadership been free to explore the possibilities, some of the younger trade unionists might have had the same opportunities as the members of Macra na Feirme (and, to a lesser extent, Muintir na Tíre and the Irish Countrywomen's Association), to go to other European countries, meet their counterparts, become aware (if not involved) in the contemporary European debate and gain the experience that such international seminars and conferences could give.

With the proposals for a Free Trade Area, however, the problem came closer to home and the position more serious. In January 1957, the OEEC working party on the possibilities of a Free Trade Area published its report, which concluded that such a FTA could be operated but that there were many open questions as to its nature.[4] A month later the British government published its own White Paper as a memorandum to the OEEC in which it was clear that the British favoured an Industrial Free Trade Area and a politically different structure from that envisaged in the Common Market of the Six. The British government, largely backed by the opposition, publicised its proposals and the British TUC, plus the great majority of industrialists, supported them. When, eventually, both the British and the Six modified their original ideas the trade union movement in Britain retreated into an attitude of extreme caution, if not hostility, about an enlarged European Economic Community.

The Irish dilemma was different. By this time the breach between the two wings of the trade union movement was being healed but it was a delicate operation and neither side wanted to antagonise the other by suggesting that support of the Free Trade Area was support for purely British interests. The trade union movement, like the government, kept hoping that, somehow, the FTA proposals would be broadened, within the scope of the OEEC, to include agriculture, prevent dumping and provide help for industries – or countries – which would be badly hit by the onset of free, unrestricted competition.

At no stage does the movement, as a whole, seem to have seriously considered opting for membership of the Common Market unless and until Britain decided to do the same. Some sections of industry were anxious to break the over-dependence on the British market but they had few counterparts on the side of Irish labour.

Individual trade unionists and educational or discussion groups such as the Liberties Study Group tried to set out the options and explore the possibilities. They invited to Ireland other trade unionists, particularly some of those in the British Labour Party involved in the Britain in Europe' group to speak at seminars, usually in Dublin.

One trade union leader who became personally interested in the advantages of Irish membership of a large, European Community was Jimmy Dunne, the outstanding leader of the small Marine Port and General Workers' Union. He took a consistently independent line in the interest of his workers throughout his relatively short life and it is not surprising to see him as a member of the executive of the Irish Council of the European Movement in 1959. Port workers are immediately affected by large-scale trade agreements and the change in traditional imports and exports which inevitably follow, but Jimmy Dunne also felt that only a multi-national organisation with both the will and the power to regulate fair trade and conditions would be in a position to control the multi-national companies to whom free trade was a passport to almost free profits and inevitable exploitation of small units – whether these be trade unions, industries or even countries. He might have had reservations about the European Economic Community but they were relatively minor compared to his deep misgivings about the proposed Free Trade Area.

The report of the third annual conference of the Irish Congress of Trade Unions, held in Cork in July 1961, is a microcosm of the views of leaders of the trade union movement about developments in European integration. They range from those violently opposed to some strongly in favour, with the majority either silent or somewhere between. Andrew Barr of the National Union of Sheet Metal Workers and Coppersmiths stated his case with some force.

> The aim of the authors of the Common Market is exactly the same as the aim of capitalists anywhere in the world. It is to make the rich richer and the poor poorer. Membership of the Common Market means as far as the Republic is concerned giving up their national sovereignty. It would mean exactly the same for Britain. . . . It is true that we need a vast extension of trade. We can only get this with the countries which have complementary economies to ours, and these are the ex-colonial countries, the countries of the Socialist world. There is the alternative to entry into the Common Market and our movement would be correct in opposing any entry into the Common Market.[5]

A sober, cautious and careful debate followed. The matter was left with the Executive Council for further talks with the government and more study and research.

The leaders of the Irish trade union movement may have been deeply concerned about the global issues which jeopardised international peace but on the evidence available it does not appear that they were particularly interested in European unity. It is only at the very end of the period under review that most of them decided to investigate the phenomenon and that, obviously, because it had become clear that Ireland might well become a part of an enlarged European community.

The Civil Service

The Irish civil service has traditionally been noted for its strength, caution and honesty. In the immediate post-war period it probably contained more raw brain power than any secular institution in the country. Admission was competitive, advancement was slow but certain. Places in the civil service were eagerly sought by the brightest of those leaving secondary schools. Boys looked forward to permanent and pensionable jobs, and girls to security, at least until such time as they might marry. Many parents were anxious to secure a place for their children, and there were very many more applicants than places available.

Under the Irish constitution, it is the government which makes decisions of policy and takes responsibility for the success or failure of such policy. The advisory role played by the civil service is not spelled out in law but by tradition. In practice it is the senior civil servants who formulate policy in many departments. There is nothing peculiarly Irish in such a situation; it is common to all countries which adopted the Westminster system of democracy and divorced the civil service from the political wing of the executive. It gives the civil servant security of tenure and independence. He is expected to accept criticisms which occasionally should be more properly directed at his political masters. The power of senior civil servants varies according to the relationship they have with their ministers. An inexperienced minister may initially rely almost completely on his departmental head. A lazy or diffident one may continue to do so indefinitely. Occasionally a powerful and able politician may establish a rapport with an outstanding civil servant and the combination will result in far-reaching and radical policies (an outstanding example was the relationship between Seán Lemass and John Leydon in the Department of Industry and Commerce and Supplies in the thirties and forties). Even when the head of the department is a man (and, with the exception of Thekla Beere in the Department of Transport and Power, from 1959-66 it always has been a man) of limited vision and mediocre talents, his staying power and capacity for obstruction give him an enormous advantage over politicians, or public opinion, if he chooses to ignore or oppose them.

One of the problems in assessing the role of the civil service is the jealously guarded tradition of secrecy. Government decisions are revealed and debated, modified, reversed or forgotten but the grounds on which they were reached are not made public. The advice of the professional civil servant remains buried in his bosom or at best sealed in the archives of his department.

The absence of access to official documents throws the student of the period back to the works of those who have been given such access. In the case of the Department of Agriculture, which was later to become deeply involved in negotiations for entry into the Community, the only available published record is the work of D. Hoctor, whose book, *The Department's Story: A History of the Department of Agriculture,*[6] mentions, and briefly explains, the FAO, OEEC, GATT and the EEC. He does not, however, deal with the negotiations about the formation of a Green Pool' (the first attempt to form a common agricultural market in the fifties) nor the bargaining that must have taken place to try and get agriculture included in the Free Trade Area.

The policy of neutrality during the Second World War had significantly reinforced the inwardness of Irish bureaucrats. Lack of money, the remnants of the colonial tradition and the political exigencies of neutrality combined to make contacts abroad impossible, except on the most formal and superficial level. It is not surprising, therefore, that no Irish-European initiatives emanated from the civil service after the war. The administrators coped with the Marshall Plan and adapted to the requirements of the Organisation for Economic Co-operation.

The fact that there was a change, at least in some departments, in the latter part of the fifties was due to two extraneous factors. The first was the blatant disadvantages for Ireland of the Free Trade Area proposed by Britain. An interdepartmental survey, carried out in late 1956 and early 1957 stated that were Irish industry, in its existing situation, to be faced with unrestricted competition, up to 60 per cent of the country's industrial workers would be thrown out of work (and unemployment then stood at 9.2 per cent of the workforce).[7] This meant that Ireland would have to march out of step with Britain, however strange this might appear to those accustomed to following the economic lead of London. A lengthy article on Ireland and the European Free Trade Area' by C. H. Murray, published in *Administration,*[8] provides an example of a senior civil servant analysing, albeit in careful terms, the change which the proposed Free Trade Area – or whatever would take its place – would force on the Irish economy.

> What all this adds up to, in short, is that, in relation to the Free Trade Area it would be foolish – and useless – for us to adopt the attitude that the world owes us a living on our own terms. . . . But, even if we obtain all reasonable concessions, the Area will, nevertheless, ultimately effect a profound sea-change in our industrial structure. Just how decisive the change will be will depend in large part on how our industrialists face up to the new situation.

The second factor was Fianna Fáil's gradual shift away from the policy of protectionism which had been used to build up Irish industry during its earlier periods in power. When Seán Lemass returned as Minister for Industry and Commerce in 1957 he dominated the political and economic scene in a manner which was exceptional. Meetings of the OEEC were entirely the province of the Tánaiste and neither de Valera as Taoiseach nor Aiken as Minister of External Affairs took any decisive part in the negotiations which had such far-reaching implications.

No single date marks the turning point between the attitude which made Irish negotiators look for a twenty-five year transition period in the context of a European Free Trade Area when bargaining in 1956-7 and that which made Ireland look for full membership of the European Community in 1961. Admittedly the economic climate had changed and the European Communities, with their established Common Agricultural Policy and the noble sentiments expressed in their Treaty, looked a more promising proposition than EFTA, but that could not be the whole story. The economic improvement was striking but not so spectacular as to change Ireland from the status of an underdeveloped' country into an equal partner of any of the Six within four years. And the European Community existed in 1956-7 although no political party or civil servant was heard to mention even associate membership as a practical possibility for Ireland. Perhaps the best clue is found in the *Report of Public Services Organisation Review Group 1966-69.*[9]

> The publication of *Economic Development*[10] suggested that the Government must in future be in a position to appraise national resources, define the principles to be followed and set the targets to be reached in the process of national economic development. The acceptance of this thesis by the Government and the issue of the First Programme for Economic Expansion was, perhaps, the most significant event in the history of the Irish civil service in the post-war period.

Once the need for a *national* plan for economic development was publicly acknowledged the planners, both political and professional, had to take into account economic developments in the rest of Europe and open up the horizons of everyone involved in the economic life of the country. Whether Ireland would have taken any step to get into Europe' as early as 1961 had not Britain indicated she was interested is extremely unlikely, but it is fair to say that having made the decision in principle, Ireland showed more enthusiasm in converting it into practice than did her sister isle.

During the period covered by this study there was no appreciable growth in the size of the Irish civil service. At the end of the war there were 25,750 civil servants and in 1960 the number had grown only to 28,100, which, considering the increase in state involvement in health, education, social welfare and public services generally was extremely modest.[11] The Department for External Affairs, for historical reasons, was at the beginning of the period particularly small.

De Valera had built up the Department with an emphasis on its purely diplomatic' role and made little or no provision for trade or economic representation. This omission may have contributed to lack of interest shown by all government departments in the economic developments inherent in the creation of the European Coal and Steel Community, even before the Economic Community and Euratom came into being.

The appointment of Seán MacBride as Minister for External Affairs in 1948 transformed the Department. Part of the relative down-grading of the Department vis-à-vis the others had been due to its lack of a separate Minister while de Valera was both head of the Government and Minister for External Affairs. It began to increase its prestige at the end of the war and the process was accelerated by the appointment of MacBride, who also ranked as the leader of a political party in the Inter-Party government. The administration of Ireland's part in the European recovery programme required an extension of the Washington office and the establishment of a new section in Dublin. MacBride presided over the setting up of a new separate trade section and began to use press attachés and information officers overseas. His own interest in the Council of Europe, the OEEC and his contacts with European statesmen brought his Department more into the limelight and this continued after the change of government when, in 1956, the United Nations delegation was established.

The Department of External Affairs did achieve during the fifties an effective servicing of the Irish delegations who attended the Council of Europe, and the briefing of Irish parliamentarians and Ministers who began to attend an increasing number of international meetings with economic and political repercussions for the country. Since neither the individual politicians nor their parties were in a position to supply background information the Department had quite a heavy task, a task, moreover, which had to be carried out with considerable tact. In the following decade the Department underwent further expansion and experienced a greater emphasis on trade and commercial contacts but during the period under review it had to concentrate on diplomatic representation abroad and discreet education, mainly of parliamentarians, at home.

Another sector of the civil service which might have been expected to play an important role in the shaping of Irish attitudes to European integration was the Department of Education. The fact that primary, secondary and vocational' education were organised on quite separate lines and seem, to an outsider at least, to have had remarkably little in common, whether in structure, the training of teachers or their curricula and examinations, was reflected in a clear internal division between the different sections in the Department of Education.

The first serious 'European' contacts of the Department of Education came through the cultural activities of the Council of Europe. (There seems to have been an agreement between the Department of External Affairs and the Department of Education that the latter should represent the country on educational matters, even though the Cultural Section of the Department of External Affairs also kept an eye on the Council of Europe.) Such contacts were, however, confined to a few senior officials and the first breakthrough for the Department came in 1956 when, for the first time, it was allowed to send officials to meetings abroad without prior sanction from the Department of Finance. The lifting of this restriction enabled officials to attend regularly at Council of Europe, OECD and UNESCO meetings which dealt with all levels of education and through such meetings to make personal contacts with their European colleagues.

> It is no exaggeration to say that these visits to the Continent and to the USA were at the root of all the reforms and innovations of the 1960s, for through them we got to know the problems and some of the answers.[12]

It would appear that membership of OECD had a wider impact than membership of the Council of Europe. A greater number of officials was involved and it covered a wider range of interests.

The vocational side of the educational system seems to have made what use it could of opportunities to travel and make contacts abroad but the secondary system, being largely independent of the state, did not do so well. Few secondary teachers got to the Continent, save at their own expense. The teachers may have been aware of their isolation but there seems to have been little they felt able to do until the dramatic changes in language and other subject-teaching came in the sixties. Even the Irish section of the European Association of Teachers, created in 1963, which was supported largely by secondary school teachers did not achieve a large membership and was effective more as a pressure group than as a mass movement of teachers.

The most influential Departments in the Irish civil service were, however, Finance, and Industry and Commerce. Ministers in other departments could undoubtedly push certain projects, even though their civil servants disliked them, but the Minister for Finance and the government as a whole was at this period dependent on the officials of the Department of Finance for the figures on which to base their policies. If Finance said the money was not there and the exchequer could not stand the cost of some innovation, that was normally the end of the matter. This connection affected the relations between Finance and External Affairs particularly in connection with European economic developments.

The most obvious difficulty arose in 1947 as a result of the July Conference on European Economic Co-operation which was attended by Seán Lemass and F. H. Boland (of the Department of External Affairs) and, at the final session, by de Valera as Taoiseach and Minister for External Affairs. Ireland's interests were handled exclusively by External Affairs for the first few months and Ronan Fanning quotes J. J. McElligott, then Secretary of the Department of Finance as being highly sceptical of the European Recovery Programme:

> We cannot expect any measure of salvation from the so-called Marshall Plan', McElligott witheringly observed in the course of a general review of economic prospects submitted to his Minister on 1 August 1948. Nor did the Department react any more enthusiastically to a Benelux proposal to the O.E.E.C. Committee of Financial Experts for a stronger central organisation. Our interests in the matter', wrote O. J. Redmond (the Assistant Secretary of the Department) to External Affairs, are obviously closely related to those of Great Britain because of the direction of our foreign trade and our position as a large sterling creditor'.[13]

Finance was clearly in favour of taking a lead from London and working very closely with Britain whereas External Affairs, regardless of the economic argument, felt it was politically unacceptable. There was considerable debate as to whether the money should be given by way of grant or loan and the manner in which the funds should be spent. In the event it was the Americans who decided that it would have to be by loan and it was the Department of External Affairs and its Minister, Seán MacBride, who won the day for Irish participation in the European programme of economic recovery. It was, however, also agreed that Ireland and Great Britain would keep in close contact about the arrangements to be made, that Ireland would continue to effect the maximum economy in expenditure of hard currencies and would not exceed the level of expenditure during the first half of 1948'.[14] This was a victory for the Department of Finance but the following months, and years, were to see disputes with other Departments, notably Industry and Commerce, about the meaning of maximum economy'.

Another example of differences of attitude to Europe of the civil service is provided by the negotiations for a European Green Pool' for agriculture. The original invitation was issued to Seán MacBride, as Minister for External Affairs, in March 1951. There was then a General Election which returned Fianna Fáil to power and the matter was left over to the new government. According to the recollection of people involved at the time, confirmed by the sources quoted by Fanning, those in External Affairs were interested in the scheme, those in the Department of Finance put on record their opinion that no useful purpose would be served so far as this country is concerned by the creation of a European organisation for the marketing of certain agricultural products" and recommended that the invitation be declined'.[15] Agriculture took the line that although they had no confidence in the future of the plan and no intention of supporting it, their representatives should attend the conference at which it would be further discussed. Finance's objections, as outlined in Whitaker's memorandum, suggested that given the difficulty of creating a single market for coal and steel in six countries of Europe, a plan for the unification of the market for a wide range of agricultural products will take a long time to come to fruition;" there were doubts, too, whether, if the plan were to fructify, the Irish agricultural industry was strong enough to compete'. The Government approved the Department of Agriculture's formula and an Irish delegation, consisting of officials of the Departments of Agriculture and External Affairs, headed by the Irish Ambassador to France, attended the Green Pool Conference in Paris in May 1953.

> Their impression, they reported to the government, was that some kind of European Green Pool" organisation will probably emerge eventually, though without the executive powers originally contemplated'. However, Finance, by now strongly backed by Agriculture, continued to argue against Irish participation, which External Affairs supported on the grounds of the Irish commitment to assist the promotion of European unity and co-operation which the government have assumed as members of the Council of Europe and O.E.E.C.' – an argument scathingly criticised in a Finance minute as reducible to a desire that we should have a finger in every pie'.[16]

The combination of the departments of Agriculture and Finance, allied to the precarious position of the government and the backing of the Ministers concerned in the cabinet were too much for External Affairs and, as the seanachaí might have said, things rested so'.

Three aspects of the attitude of the Department of Finance ought to be noted here. The first, and most important, is the change which came over the Department in the mid-fifties. This has been popularly associated with the appointment of T. K. Whitaker as Secretary in May 1956, but Whitaker himself underwent a significant change. It is epitomised in two articles – in his article The Finance Attitude', published in 1953[17] he shows the Department of Finance as the guardian of public funds, opposed to economic innovation and the bastion of the philosophical legacy of the old British civil service; in 1961, in The Civil Service and Development',[18] he describes the evolution of the Department's role and its expansion which included a special division whose responsibility is to seek out ways and means of advancing economic growth and to develop ideas and projects to the point at which they can be placed with the appropriate department and agency . . .'. Finance would still keep a close watch on the purse strings but would also concern itself with broader issues, both national and international.

The second aspect of the Department of Finance which should be noted is that its Ministers during this period (with the exception, at times, of Patrick McGilligan) seem to have been in harmony with the attitude of their civil servants.

Thirdly, it has been often argued that the delay of twelve years between Ireland's application to join the European communities and her accession in 1973 was essential to prepare the country for the experience. How much more so the delay from the fifties? Perhaps the officials were right to save us from the possibilities of the Green Pool' and the dangers of cutting the links with Whitehall. They certainly assumed that the economic fate of Ireland was inexorably bound to Britain forever.

The Department of Industry and Commerce also wielded considerable power, partly because of its function in controlling many of the complex trading regulations which were a legacy of the war-years and of the protectionist policy of the early years of the state and partly because of the energy and influence of Seán Lemass who was the Minister responsible for a long and important period, and of the Secretary, John Leydon, another formidable figure. According to the recollection of an official in that Department, concern was felt at what seemed to be the excessive British influence in the commercial and business life of Ireland: There was, for instance, the spectacle of subsidiaries of British manufacturing companies who were permitted to sell in Ireland only, as the British and export markets were reserved to the parent company in Britain.[19]

The publication of the report of the OEEC Working Party in January 1957 came just when it was painfully obvious that Ireland needed to make some changes to improve her economic and trading position. The envisaged industrial Free Trade Area never came into being and when the split into Common Market and the Free Trade Association came Ireland found herself isolated from both.

Much thought was devoted during the period 1959 to 1961, at Lemass's insistence as Taoiseach, to ways of overcoming this isolation. In particular, the possibility of special bilateral trade arrangements with Britain and the question of joining EFTA were studied. The Secretaries of the four main economic Departments – Finance, Industry and Commerce, Agriculture and External Affairs – met frequently as a committee reporting on these matters to a cabinet committee chaired by Mr. Lemass. The correspondence which passed between the four Secretaries – particularly Finance and Industry and Commerce – was intended also for the eyes of the Taoiseach and other Ministers on the cabinet committee and may be presumed to have had some influence on policy.[20]

Contradictory pressures within the civil service made it difficult to formulate a united view which could be put publicly to the Oireachtas or even advanced at the negotiating table. On the one hand there was the fear of what free trade would do to Irish industry, coupled with a feeling that it was inevitable in the long run. On the other hand there was a desire to maintain the special trading relationship with Britain, struggling with the growing realisation that Irish agriculture and some small sectors of Irish industry needed an entry to wider markets to expand and develop. The result was relative stagnation until the combination of Seán Lemass's decision to change course and the pressure of external developments forced Ireland to evolve a coherent policy in line with the choice to seek membership of the European Communities.

The Business Community

Any comparative study of Ireland and her European neighbours during this period reveals a distinct difference in the volume of public pronouncements made by business' in Ireland and in Europe. In most countries those firms which saw opportunities in a large common market actively supported moves towards European integration, while those which feared competition on the home market or were in decline opposed them. In Britain, in particular, there was considerable support from industry for a policy of joining the European Communities but Irish industry and enterprise said relatively little.

There were three main reasons for the scarcity of statements from Irish businessmen. Firstly, many Irish companies were subsidiaries, particularly of British firms, and all policy statements were normally made from the parent company in London or elsewhere. Secondly, the great majority of Irish-owned firms had been created to supply the home-market and owed their success to extensive protection on that market. They were therefore fearful about the effects of free trade even though they would also have had misgivings about being totally isolated were Ireland to be refused entry into any trading group. Such double apprehensions must have inhibited any nailing of their colours to the mast. Thirdly, there was the character and personality of the people involved. Irish business was, by European standards, very small scale and the men who ran it were accustomed to direct contact with their public representatives, or even their Ministers, when they wanted to put forward their interests or canvass political support for their enterprise. With the exception of a few big firms Irish companies were family owned and managed and still mainly in the hands of the founders. There was little opportunity for the preparation of submissions or public statements and no back-up research staff to produce the supporting evidence for such statements or submissions.

An attempt to find evidence of business attitudes in the records of the Federated Union of Employers confirms this view and the meagre gleanings from the annual report of the Federation of Irish Manufacturers, referred to in Chapter Four, show how difficult it was, even for the representative organisations of industry and employers, to produce the kind of public pressure engendered by similar bodies in Britain and elsewhere.

There is a change from the absolute silence of the early years to the relative loquacity of 1958 onwards and the list of the group members of the Irish Council of the European Movement in 1958 shows that quite a few individual companies had become involved. Most of this was due to the pressure of external events but some was due to the emergence of a new generation of technically qualified managers. They were therefore both more export-oriented and more anxious to explore the wider economic possibilities of a change in trading relationships in Europe. Furthermore, the development of the state-sponsored bodies, many of which were, for all practical purposes, straight-forward trading enterprises, made it possible for their executives to play a very important part in the forming of attitudes in the business sector. Such men were sometimes former civil servants and therefore had channels of communication to their erstwhile colleagues not enjoyed by those in the private sector. Others were career businessmen who found outlets which would have been denied them in the family-dominated structure of much of the private sector. Lt. General M. J. Costello of the Irish Sugar Company has already been mentioned in Chapter Seven but there was also C. S. Andrews of Córas Iompair Éireann (and earlier of Bord na Móna) and in 1959 the creation of the Shannon Free Airport Development Company was hailed as a means of injecting foreign capital and know-how' into Irish industry. Its first general manager, Brendan O'Regan, was prominent as an advocate of Irish involvement in European economic co-operation.

Irish industry, and Irish business generally, naturally reacted to developments on the European scene in what it saw as its own interest. In this it was not very different from its European counterpart. The scale, and structure of Irish enterprise, however, made it particularly dependent on British policy and vulnerable to external pressures. In the absence of any radical visionary leader who might have seen the presence of Ireland in Europe as an economic leap forward, it must be said that the business community did stand aloof until events made it necessary to get involved. It should also be explained that many foresighted people in private and state-sponsored enterprise saw the debate on possible membership of EFTA or the EEC as an opportunity to bring about changes in the Irish economy which were desirable in themselves. In 1961 M. J. Haughey, chairman of Córas Tráchtála, emphasised that the creation of a Committee on Industrial Organisation, the development of industrial processing of agricultural produce and the search for more diversified markets to end the over-dependence on the UK (which took more than seventy-five per cent of all Irish exports) were all essential to the survival and expansion of Irish industry.[21] The attitudes of the Irish business community to Irish involvement in European integration were cautious and pragmatic but not, on the whole, hostile.

The Verdict

In 1972 the Irish people approved, by a decisive majority, the proposal to join the European Community. Their endorsement of the decision originally made in 1961 was of course influenced by the events of the intervening years. But the decision of 1961, once taken, itself had an impact on the developments which followed and brought new actors on stage and a new direction to the course of Irish history.

In the widespread examination of the kind of Community in which Ireland finds herself in the eighties two lines of enquiry might repay some study. Firstly, what kind of preparation were the years 1948-61 for the choice of full membership of the European Communities? What kind of reception would Ireland have received in Brussels and the Chancelleries of Europe had she proposed a special role for herself from the beginning? How would the Europeans have reacted to a country which offered herself as a link with the sterling area, a back-door to the British connection and a catalyst for the Community by becoming a seventh member? There is no evidence that such a course occurred to those in political or diplomatic circles. Ireland did not see herself as taking the initiative in the process of European integration. Yet the movement towards European integration either inspired or accelerated initiatives taken in Ireland which were to have profound effects on the country in the coming decades.

Secondly, one might wonder what the advocates of European unity in the post-war era would have thought of the Community as it exists today? Those who opposed (or advocated) accession in 1972 are still mainly available to give their views. But what of the pioneers? Would they find it strange that a full member of the European Community, with a seat in the Council of Ministers and members in a directly-elected European Parliament still, to a large extent, regards 'Europe' as foreign? Would they be suprised that Brussels is best known as a source of arbitrary largesse or hardship? Would they expect Irish leaders to have persuaded the people that there is a particular contribution which can be made on behalf of Ireland for the good of the citizens of the entire Community? Would they be disappointed that our membership has been of a peculiarly passive nature, though this doesn't apply only in Ireland? Perhaps they would have been realistic enough to accept that it takes both time and a pressure of events (unfortunately, usually a common danger) to inspire loyalty or emotions to a new institution. A decade, or even two, is not a very long time in which to generate fealty or affection, unless the driving force is exceptional.

★ ★ ★

Preparation for Europe during the period under review may have been haphazard but it withstood considerable strain in the succeeding years. Despite the contrast between Ireland and the six original members, the Irish government, without any appreciable note of dissent from the Irish people, decided to apply for full rather than associate membership of the European Communities in 1961. Without any particular sign of encouragement on the part of the Six or notable enthusiasm from the other applicants, government and people remained generally firm about membership in the years which followed. So what was special about the experience of these years? Four features stand out. Firstly, there is the Irish understanding of 'European integration' and of European Federalism. Secondly, there is the cauldron of internal pressures, sometimes warming towards Europe and sometimes cooling. Thirdly, there is the pull of external forces which drew the country closer to the mainland. Finally, there are the many important domestic changes which were accentuated and accelerated by the possibility of becoming part of the European bloc – changes which their proposers showed no reluctance to justify under the requirements for membership of a European Community even if they were more interested in transforming Ireland than in joining Europe. It was a new and sophisticated version of the philosophy of Sinn Féin.

Integration

The term 'integration' was understood by the actors on the Irish scene between 1948 and 1961 in a particular way. The term is used, even by sociologists and political scientists, to describe both a state of unity and a process of unification. However, people can be in favour of the process without really desiring the ultimate state. The process rather than the ultimate state was considered of immediate relevance and this for three reasons. Firstly, all the speeches, letters and articles of the time considered European integration to be an organic, living development and the various shifts of emphasis and strategy coming from the 'integrationists' on the mainland confirmed, in Irish minds, the inherent uncertainty about the final result. Secondly, there was a constant undercurrent of feeling that the Irish state was not yet quite ready to throw in its lot with big partners in a political and economic undertaking of remarkable breadth and sophistication. Thirdly, the British attitude, whether in accord with the Irish proponents' views or not, was still relevant as to how far it would be possible for Ireland, particularly with her emotional and political involvement with Northern Ireland and her economic dependence on Britain, to enter a European alliance.

These three reasons are very clearly seen in the context of Ireland and the Council of Europe. While the Council was originally proposed as a 'parliament of Europe', it had become, by the time it reached the stage of signature and ratification, a consultative assembly, with a weak secretariat and a strong council of ministers – just the kind of organisation advocated by the functionalists and deplored by the federalists.

When the spotlight switched to the OEEC in 1956-7 it was a recognition that integration was then being stated in economic terms. Pragmatic interests in economic co-operation, however, soon reached their limits and it became obvious that, in order to achieve real integration or even make further economic progress, a political commitment would have to be made by the statesmen and politicians (and by the civil servants who translated their ideas into reality at the bargaining table). A political dimension had also to be acknowledged by those who influenced their own sectors of the national community and whose voice carried weight with public opinion. Irish eyes then turned to the possibilities of the European Economic Community and public interest in the Council of Europe declined from that time. The debates in the Council of Europe, however, show the fears of the Irish politicians for the fragile economy and the defensive aspects of their nationalism when others issued a clarion call to integration. Finally, the quarrels of some of the Irish representatives with their British colleagues in the Assembly are reported in the same volume as speeches by them which are almost identical with British Conservative policy. It is noticeable that most of those who favoured closer links with Europe (again with Seán MacBride as an exception) were those who were least pre-occupied with a running battle, even a verbal one, with the United Kingdom, but were more concerned with breaking the emotional relationship between the two islands. Yet even this attitude meant a glance over the shoulder at what was happening in Britain and it was always clear that it would be easier to avoid a choice between declarations of intent to pursue European integration and loyalty to the idea of the ultimate unification of Ireland if both parts of the island could be integrated together. This depended on Britain.

Decision-making, particularly in economic matters, was never fully in the hands of a small state and difficulties with the Anglo-Irish trade agreements and attempts to open up trade with the US made this abundantly plain to the Irish. Loyalty to the nation-state, however, was a different matter and loyalty to an integrated Europe was always put forward by those in favour as an extension rather than diminution of this attribute. The growth of self-confidence which accompanied the expansion of Irish interests in the fifties helped to alter the colour of Irish-British co-operation in a European context. It is apparent in almost all the speeches of the period, particularly in those reported in the news-sheets of the Department of External Affairs, that it had become the accepted wisdom to proclaim publicly and frequently that the problem of Northern Ireland would never be solved by war or coercion. Only the members of Sinn Féin or the IRA dissented. Since Britain was the only possible member of the proposed enlarged Community of Ten in 1961 with whom Ireland could conceivably have cause for armed disagreement, this attitude was an important contributor to the express and implied 'no war' European Community.

Ireland's careful distinction between membership of NATO and membership of a European Community which might, at a future date, call upon its members to rally to their mutual defence or to the defence of one of their members, is not as arcane as some impatient observers might feel. NATO, as a military alliance, was declined by the Irish governments in the forties mainly because of its implications for Northern Ireland and national sovereignty. The distinction between neutrality and non-alignment might have been hazy in many minds but general sentiment was against membership of NATO or a similar military organisation. The lack of enthusiasm displayed by France for her multi-national military commitments and the ambivalence of British and French moves in the whole field of mutual defence, plus the neutralist tendencies of some of the left-wing parties in the European Community, made it easy for Irish leaders to agree, wholeheartedly, to a non-belligerence between members and, in principle, to some form of mutual help should one of the Community members be attacked from without. Defence was not, after all, in the Treaty of Rome; NATO was still the preferred weapon of the British; the smaller nations were unlikely to agree to an alternative military force which could be used for purposes of aggression; and the history of the fifties made it clear that a European Defence Community raised as many problems in the Six as it might have done in Ireland. For these reasons, Irish leaders saw no difficulty in reconciling their policy of present neutrality with a promise of eventual succour – should it be required.

Why, apart from the question of defence, did federalism, which had been advocated as a possible solution for the Irish question as long ago as the Twenties, not receive much consideration as a desirable form of European integration? The diversity, so dear to federalist hearts, and the principle of subsidiarity which was implicit in their doctrine, should have made the theory attractive in Ireland. Some of the federalist faith was indeed preached during this period, but rarely explicitly, and never with full vigour. Was this because the Irish protagonists preferred to follow what was accepted as the British habit of not nailing down policies to identifiable political theories, always leaving an ambiguous blur around the edges? Did those who suggested a federalist solution for Ireland itself fear to complicate the delicate situation further by adding a European dimension? Did those who would have considered the principle in regional (i.e., European) terms fear to become embroiled in the national issue?

It is the silence in this case which is most intriguing. This aspect of the study served as a warning not to try and fit the Irish experience, with hindsight, into a model of classification which would have been neat rather than valid.

Internal pressures

Another strange silence is that of opponents of the idea of Irish involvement in European integration. De Valera and the Fianna Fáil party, which was the most articulate group of Cassandras in the early days of the Council of Europe, whenever political integration was mooted, were nevertheless always in favour of 'strong and close co-operation' and, if some term must be found, of a sort of neo-functionalist development in western Europe. During the period under review, integration, even under other names, was rather like democracy, peace, economic progress and happy family life – all were in favour in principle, only on matters of practice were there strong differences. The opponents who were to come to the fore in later years saw no real 'danger' during the fifties. They either considered the enthusiasm of the proponents of Irish involvement in European integration as wildly unrealistic, or assumed that Europe would not want the addition of a country as economically vulnerable as Ireland. Some of them also relied on the inherent self-interest of politicians and civil servants to resist any change to a system which would introduce a new set of rules and inevitably curtail their ability to allocate resources, awards and patronage of different kinds. They ignored the signals picked up by the farming community, followed by the business world and those with the political acumen to read the omens.

The lack of interest which was noted in the trade union movement and Labour Party, after initial approval of the Council of Europe, is even reflected, over twenty years later, in the policy statement adopted by the Administrative Council of the Labour Party on *Ireland and the European Community* and presented to a special national conference of the Labour Party on 8, 9 December 1978 prior to the direct elections to the European Parliament in June 1979. In discussing the 'Community and the Citizen' the document says 'The Community *can no longer be seen as a distant and irrelevant institution in Brussels'* (p. 6; italics mine). Did the feeling that European integration was irrelevant to Ireland enable the Irish Labour Party to avoid making their anti-Market stand an emotional, personal commitment and therefore help them to accept the decision of the referendum in 1973? Such speculation is outside the chronological framework of this study but the comment rings true with regard to the attitudes of the fifties.

There was also the matter of covert opposition to the whole concept of open frontiers, free trading and the political and social implications which followed from long-term economic planning and close links with the experiment of the European Communities. Because this sprang from a number of different and sometimes contradictory reasons or emotions it is almost impossible to chart its course.

Certainly it flavours some of the recalls to ancient verities issued occasionally by businessmen, clergy or local politicians at that time and it is remembered by many who were actively engaged in promoting discussion on both economic and European affairs during the period.

The extent to which increased and better communications affected the attitudes firstly of the elites and subsequently of quite large sectors of public opinion, was striking. In the summing up of his work, *Europe in Question*, Harrison states that 'in societies forced to adapt as a result of the impact of technology, foreign threat or influence, or natural disaster, the ability to recognise new assets may be one of the major political skills, a factor which may be favourable to an integration strategy led by a powerful member elite or elites.'[1] The possibility of union with Europe as an alternative to increasing dependence on Britain in a deteriorating economic climate was certainly seized on by members of Irish elites towards the end of the period but this alternative could never have been disseminated had personal contacts with European colleagues not been dramatically increased, the means of internal communication on a national level been vastly improved and the dependence on British sources of news and comment been considerably reduced. The manipulative skill, particularly of Seán Lemass, required the backing of a consensus on the home front that Ireland should seriously investigate the possibilities of the new European situation. The changes which took place between 1948 and 1961 in Irish society were reflected in and accelerated by the changes in publishing and broadcasting over the same period.

External forces

The external forces which led much of post-war Europe, through a mixture of self-interest and idealism, to consider integration applied also to Ireland. The self-interest was fed by US encouragement, Soviet threats and the voracious demands of technological development and economic inter-dependence.

Were it not for US insistence on inter-European co-operation in the sharing of the aid made available for reconstruction after the war there would have been no OEEC and the drive towards economic integration would have been far weaker. Irish politicians and civil servants were naturally first affected by the terms on which aid was given but, once part of the organisation into which they had virtually been forced by the combination of home needs and available foreign aid, they then became convinced of the advantages of economic co-operation – albeit at an inter-governmental level.

The Soviet threat was cushioned for Ireland by the thought of the existence of the rest of Europe, Great Britain, the US forces in Europe, and the Irish Sea. This perhaps also explains further the special Irish attitude to defence. It also marks one of the very definite divergences between the Irish position and that of her neighbours.

The requirements of technological development could not be met by the Irish economy. Outside capital, skills and markets were needed and Ireland could only look East or West. Because the Irish market was so small American commercial interests were only attracted to Ireland as an investment base for the UK and Europe and if access to these could be assured, were prepared to supply finance and management. The search for new investment, new techniques and new outlets all combined therefore to turn Ireland towards Europe.

In the extraordinary event that Ireland had experienced no internal impulse or no other external stimulus to consider the implications of European integration she would have been forced to do so once it had been raised by her powerful neighbour. It is an indication of the strength of the other pressures that, firstly, any debate took place in Ireland and then, that attitudes and policies were adopted which were different from those of the UK. The two countries reached the same decision in 1961; the timing was largely dictated by Britain but the background and the expectations and fears behind the decision were quite different in each country.

Domestic changes

The protagonists for change in Irish society frequently used the possibility of a close link with Europe as a lever with which to gain support for their policies in other spheres.

This was most marked in two sectors: firstly, those, many of whom were in the Irish Council of the European Movement, who wanted a change of outlook, a breaking with the obsessions of the past and a possibility of new and wider horizons for the future. If the thrust towards Europe had not existed they would have had to create it and in the earlier years covered by this study that is virtually what they did.

The second sector included those, particularly in the state-sponsored bodies, in agriculture and in some sectors of industry, who wanted to modernise Irish management, methods of production and farming and used the threat of European competition and the carrot of European markets to try and galvanise their colleagues, partners, bureaucrats and government into accepting necessary reforms.

The reasons for the change in outlook are complex. The creation of new physical links with the rest of Europe through the development of Aer Lingus routes, the easing of regulations allowing civil servants to attend conferences abroad, the advent of a national television station, have to be mentioned (even if in low key) as well as the acceptance of the concept of economic planning and a philosophical search for a European alternative to the traditional obsession with all things British. The very low Irish standard of competence in modern European languages was probably as relevant to the attitude of many Irish leaders of opinion as any ideological commitment to neo-functionalism or plain pragmatism as proposed mainly by British politicians.

The policy of attracting foreign (i.e. other than British) industries to set up in Ireland was only beginning but it was to affect Irish awareness of Europe in the industrial field in the sixties – both as a market and a competitor. The Danes were approximately twelve years ahead in this field but they did not feel the need to express their identity in a

European context, sheltered as they were by the Scandinavian grouping and enjoying relations with Britain which were untouched by historical and economic complications of the kind endured in Ireland.

If there were doubts on the Irish side, the reception given by the European Community to the Irish application for full membership is an indication that others too had reservations. This study stops with Ireland's formal application for membership of the EEC under Article 237 which was presented to the Council on 31 July 1961. The Taoiseach informed the Dáil on the following day, and the ambiance in which Irish opinion developed was changed. It is, however, relevant to note that the terms of acknowledgment sent to Ireland differed significantly from those sent to the United Kingdom and Denmark; this provoked an immediate flurry of activity, during which the Secretaries of the Departments of Finance and External Affairs made a tour of the capitals of the Six urging acceptance of Ireland as a full rather than associate member. This should be read as a further proof that the decision to apply, although somewhat sudden at the end, was wholehearted and that the known differences of opinion among the governments of the member states acted as a spur rather than a brake on the Irish government's eagerness to join.

After all the explanations of the special circumstances created by the historical, social and economic environment in the preceding pages, it must be asked if Irish attitudes had anything in common with those of any other European country. As the extracts from the files of the EYC and the records of Muintir na Tíre showed, there were many issues which aroused a common response from Irish and continental people who faced them from similar backgrounds. Nor were the Irish alone in being vague about which point of the scale they should choose as their preferred degree of integration.

> It could be asserted that the limited response to European integration on the part of the European is partially due to the uncertainty of its general perspective and the lack of a convincing and articulate philosophy. . . . The lim-

> ited *participation* of the European in European integration may have deeper causes and it may not be simply a matter of more and better information.[2]

The dichotomy which existed in Irish minds was shared by many others.

There is also an analogy to be drawn between the Irish attempt to move from post-colonial economic dependence to a limited form of inter-dependence in an integrated European Community and that of countries which had experienced foreign occupation, either during or after the war and were looking for some of the same safeguards – albeit at a more rapid pace. Only Britain, Sweden and Switzerland were in completely separate categories. The differences were of degree and of timing and might have been less had there been any serious and reasonably widespread interest in the Irish situation on the part of the committed Europeans.

The decision to seek full membership of the European Communities in 1961, however mixed the motives, was accompanied by considerable cultural, social and economic changes. Some of these were merely coincidental but others facilitated or flowed from the decision. The formal request to join the European Community was seen both as an attempt at fuller independence and a move towards closer integration. It is this paradox which makes the background of Ireland's first application to become a member of the EEC of special interest. The political implications may have been imperfectly understood at the time (indeed it is occasionally revealed that they are not yet fully apparent to all the political leaders of even the founding member states) but the psychological effects were striking. The period from 1948 to 1961 was one of trial and transition for Irish society. The decision to look for a place in the company of the nations of western Europe was an act of both faith and hope – in Ireland itself and in the European Community.

Appendix

International Organisations

Organisation	*Founded*	*Ireland Joined*
Council of Europe (C. of E.)	May 1949	1949 (Inter-Party)
Economic Co-operation (Act) Administration (ECA)	US (Legislation) and Organisation governing bi-lateral agreements of the European Recovery Programme 1948-1951	1948 (Inter-Party)
European Coal and Steel Community (ECSC)	1952	1973 (Fianna Fáil)
European Economic Community (EEC)	1958	1973 (FF)
European Atomic Energy Community (Euratom)	1958	1973 (FF)
European Payments Union (EPU)	Est. 1950 by OEEC and ECA	1950 (Inter-Party)
European Free Trade Association (EFTA)	1958	—
Food & Agricultural Organisation (FAO)	1945	1946 (FF)
General Agreement on Tariffs and Trade (GATT)	1948	1967 (FF) (Enjoyed observer status in earlier years)
International Labour Office (later 'Organisation') (ILO)	1919 under League of Nations – Affiliated to UN 1946	1923 (Cumann na nGaedheal)
International Monetary Fund (IMF)	1945 (as a result of Bretton Woods Agreement 1944)	1957 (FF)
North Atlantic Treaty Organisation (NATO)	1949	—
Organisation for European Economic Co-operation (OEEC)	1948	1948 (Inter-Party)
Organisation for European Co-operation and Development (OECD)	1960 (Successor of OEEC)	1960 (FF)
United Nations Organisation (UNO)	1945	1955 (Inter-Party)
Western European Union (WEU)	1955	—
World Health Organisation (WHO)	1948	1948 (Inter-Party)

Notes

Introduction

[1]Dáil Reports. Vol. 302: 1683.

[2]Haas, E. B., 'The Study of Regional Integration: Reflections on the Joy and Anguish of Pre-theorising'; *International Organisation* XXIV, 4, 1970, p. 627; quoted by R. J. Harrison in 'Europe in Question'; p. 88.

Ireland in the Post-War World

[1]Quoted from 'Documents on German Foreign Policy, 1918-1945', Series D, Washington D.C., 1949-1964, by T. Ryle Dwyer in *Irish Neutrality and the U.S.A. 1939-1947*, Gill & Macmillan, Dublin, 1977.

[2]*Ulster at the Crossroads* by Terence O'Neill, Faber & Faber, London, 1969 with an introduction by John Cole, assistant editor of *The Guardian* from which this quotation is taken.

[3]*The Irish – A Character Study* by Seán Ó Faoláin. Devin-Adair Company, New York, 1949, pp. 95-6.

[4]See *The Blueshirts* by Maurice Manning. Gill & Macmillan, Dublin, 1970.

[5]*A History of the Irish Working Class,* by P. Beresford Ellis, Gollancz, London, 1972, p. 292.

[6]*Irish Neutrality and the U.S.A. 1939-1947* by T. Ryle Dwyer. Published Gill & Macmillan, Dublin, 1977, p. 2.

[7]*Ireland Since the Famine* by F. S. L. Lyons. Published Collins/Fontana, pp. 557-8.

1948–51

[1]*Tribute to a Great European – J. H. Retinger.* Published Centre Europeènne de la Culture, p. 45.

[2]Letter from Senator Douglas to Dr. Retinger, 19 June 1948. Original in Archives of College of Europe, Bruges. The discussion in the Senate actually took place in August 1948. (See *Reports of Seanad Éireann,* Vol 35; 747-761 for James Douglas contribution, followed by that of Eleanor Butler, *ibid.* 761-771.)

[3]Copy of letter from Retinger to 'His Grace, The Archbishop of Dublin', 19 September 1948. *Ibid.*

[4]Dáil Reports. 112; 900-931 and 947-1024.

[5]Dáil Reports. 112: 1022-1023.

[6]Excerpt by Ernst Haas in *International Political Communities,* published Anchor Books 1966, pp. 93-110.

[7]Dáil Debates. 62: 2774–81.

[8]Annual Report of Secretary of the Federation of Irish Manufacturers Ltd., Kevin McCourt, for 1948, p. 17.

[9]Dáil Reports: 114: 323-6. A more formal reply was returned to the official invitation, with a rider to the effect that the existence of Partition was a continuing threat to the peace of both Britain and Ireland.

[10]Dáil Reports. 117: 748.

[11]*The Irish Times.* 'Profile of the Countess of Wicklow', 28 October 1978.

[12]Irish Delegates to the First Consultative Assembly of the Council of Europe 1949. *Delegates:* Deputy Norton (Tánaiste and Minister for Industry and Commerce), Deputy Everett (Minister for Posts and Telegraphs), Deputy de Valera (Leader of the Opposition), Deputy MacEntee; *Substitutes:* Deputy Aiken, Deputy Sweetman, Senator Crosbie, Senator Finan. From *Official Records of Council of Europe.*

[13]*The Irish Times,* 12 August 1949.

[14]*Europe in Question* by R. J. Harrison. Allen & Unwin, London, 1974. Chapter on 'The Functionalist Approach', p. 29.

[15]Official Reports of Council of Europe Consultative Assembly. O.R. Part One: 1st Sitting: 10/8/1949, p. 7.

[16]*To Katanga and Back. A U.N. Case History* by Conor Cruise O'Brien. Hutchinson, London, 1962, p. 14.

[17]Reports of Council of Europe. Part One: 1st Sitting: 10/8/1949, p. 19.

[18]Quoted in *Éire/Ireland,* Bulletin of Dept. of External Affairs: No. 136, 19/5/1952.

[19]*Éire/Ireland,* No. 229: 12/4/1954.

[20]Official Reports of Council of Europe Consultative Assembly: 10 August–8 September 1949, p. 238.

[21]O.R. Part One: Sittings 1-5. Second Session of Council of Europe Consultative Assembly: 1950, pp. 277-84.

[22]Dáil Reports. 122: 1590-1607.

[23]Dáil Reports. 122: 1607-8.

[24]Official Reports of C. of E. Vol IV. 3rd Ordinary Session: 1951, p. 835.

[25]*The Irish Times,* 7 March 1951.

The Trough of Depression 1952–57

[1]*Ireland Since the Famine* by F. S. L. Lyons. Published Collins–Fontana, p. 591.

[2]Official Reports. Council of Europe. 4th Ordinary Session. Part 2, 1952. Vol. III, pp. 404-6.

[3]*Church and State in Modern Ireland – 1923-1970* by J. H. Whyte. Published: Gill & Macmillan, Dublin, 1971.

[4]For a full, albeit committed, account, see 'Methodes et Mouvements pour Unir l'Europe', Bulletin de la Centre Europeènne de la Culture. Geneva, May 1958.

[5]*The Leader,* 28 August 1954.

[6]Dáil Reports. 152: 540.

[7]*Sunday Press,* 20 May 1956. This Seminar was opened by the Minister for External Affairs, Liam Cosgrave, and Seán MacBride was also a speaker. The President of UCG, Monsignor Padraig de Brun, presided over the main session and there was a considerable number of 'mainland' Europeans present, as well as a contingent from Northern Ireland and Great Britain.

[8]Conversation with senior civil servant who had been actively involved with the negotiations.

Free Trade versus Common Market 1957–9

[1]*Economic Growth in Ireland – The Experience Since 1947* by Kieran A. Kennedy and Brendan R. Dowling. Gill & Macmillan in association with The Economic & Social Research Institute, Dublin, 1975, pp. 214-230.

[2]*The Irish Press,* 8 May 1957.

[3]*Currency and Central Banking in Ireland 1922-1960* by Maurice Moynihan. Published Gill & Macmillan in association with the Central Bank of Ireland, Dublin, 1975, p. 438.

[4]*The Irish Times,* 3 July 1957 and Dáil Reports, 163: 629-630.

[5]Dáil Report. 163: 633-667.

[6]*The Statist,* 9 January 1958. Article entitled 'Ireland and the E.F.T.A.'.

[7]Official Reports, Council of Europe, 29 April – 3 May 1957, Vol. 1, p. 104.

[8]All Irish papers, 9 January 1959. Front page heading, *The Irish Times:* 'Ireland Supports British Free Trade Plan – Effort to Avoid Crisis'.

[9]T. K. Whitaker, 'From Protection to Free Trade – The Irish Experience', *Administration,* Winter 1973, Vol. 21, No. 4, p. 416.

[10]*Programme for Economic Expansion,* November 1958, pp. 37-38.

[11]European Economic Conference organised by the Irish Council of the European Movement in Dublin, 20 July 1959. Pamphlet published by ICEM, p. 20.

[12]A valuable summary called, 'Broadcasting in Ireland prior to Establishment of the Authority' may be found in Radio Telefís Éireann First Annual Report for the ten months ended 31 March 1961.

Taking the Plunge 1960–61

[1]'Irish Times Review and Annual – January 2, 1961', Garret FitzGerald's review of the economy during 1960.

[2]Initial proceedings taken in 1958. Decision of the Court given 1 July 1961. Ref: Yearbook of European Convention of Human Rights: IV, p. 438. The preliminary objections and points of procedure raised by both the Commission and the Irish Government were ruled on 14 November 1960 and the public hearings held in Strasbourg, 7-11 April 1961 so the case spread over four years, with most legal attention being paid (after the initial flurry of the first application) in 1960 and 1961.

[3]'Irish Times Review and Annual 1962'.

[4]*Economic Activity in Ireland – A Study of Two Open Economies.* Edited by Norman J. Gibson and John E. Spencer. Gill and Macmillan, 1977, see p. 142.

[5]Dáil Reports. 176: 567.

[6]Dáil Reports. 179: 983–4.

[7]Dáil Reports. 182: 766.

[8]Dáil Reports. 186: 11.

[9]Dáil Reports. 189: 298.

[10]Dáil Reports. 190: 179.

[11]Dáil Reports. 190: 623.

[12]*European Economic Community*, laid by the Government before each House of the Oireachtas, 30 June 1961. Dublin: Stationery Office.

[13]Dáil Reports. 191: 206.

[14]*The Irish Times,* 10 May 1961.

[15]*The Irish Times,* 23 May 1961.

[16]*The Irish Times* headline, 5 June 1961.

The Media

[1]*Irish Independent,* 27 January 1957.

[2]30 January 1957. Law Students Debating Society of Ireland: the Auditor was Denis Corboy, Chairman – Garret FitzGerald.

[3]*Forty Years of Irish Broadcasting,* Maurice Gorham. Dublin, Talbot Press, 1965, p. 221.

[4]*Éire/Ireland,* No. 214, 21/12/1953.

[5]*Éire/Ireland,* No. 217, 18/1/1954.

[6]*Éire/Ireland,* No. 548, 6/11/1961.

[7]*Éire/Ireland,* No. 538, 31/7/1961.

Voluntary Organisations and Universities

[1]Letter from Retinger to H. E. the Irish Ambassador. Preso la Santa Sede, Villa Spada, Via Giocomo Medici, Roma. 11 March 1952. Archives of College of Europe, Bruges.

[2]Correspondence concerned in the files of Archives of College of Europe, Bruges. Foley subsequently became an M.P., Minister in the Wilson government, and then involved in overseas development in the Commission of the European Community.

[3]List of member organisations later circulated to members: Boy Scouts of Ireland, Catholic Boy Scouts of Ireland, Catholic Women's Federation of Secondary School Unions, Catholic Young Men's Society, Comhairle le Leas Óige, Dublin Institute of Catholic Sociology, Dublin University Association for International Affairs, Girls' Friendly Society, Irish Association of Catholic University Students, Irish Countrywomen's Association, Irish Girl Guides, Irish Students' Association, Macra na Feirme, Muintir na Tíre and Tuairim.

[4]Minutes and letter in Comhairle le Leas Óige file; letter received 1 July 1952.

[5]*Towards A European Government* by Henri Brugmans. Pamphlet published by European Youth Campaign. Paris, 1953; p. 9.

[6]For the whole debate see Seanad Éireann Reports Vol. 35; 747—772.

[7]Published in *Studies* and reprinted in pamphlet form, 'Recent Economic Development in Europe' — Dublin. Irish Council of the European Movement, 1959.

[8]Irish Review and Annual 1959, published by *The Irish Times*, January 1960.

[9]*The Leader*, editorial 9 May 1959.

[10]'Ireland and Europe'. *The Leader* 18 July 1959, p. 7.

[11]*Irish Press* report of a speech by M. J. Costello to the National University of Ireland Club in London, 20 October 1958.

Rural Organisations

[1]*Ireland Since the Famine* F. S. L. Lyons, Fontana, 1978. Note on p. 561.

[2]Interview with Seán FitzMaurice in *Regeneration – Rural Resurgence in Ireland;* p. 161.

[3]International Federation of Agricultural Producers; World organisation with a strong European Committee: 'Comite des Organisations de Producteurs Agricoles', COPA and 'Confederation Europeenne des Agriculteurs'.

[4]Recollections of Seán Healy, first Secretary of the NFA, given verbally to the author.

[5]Muintir na Tíre Guide (1958).

[6]*European Youth Campaign in Ireland.* Explanatory leaflet carried extracts from the address of His Holiness, Pope Pius XII, delivered to delegates of the Second International Congress of the European Union of Federalists in Rome, 11 November, 1948. This was extensively used by the member organisations, including Muintir na Tíre.

[7]*An Appraisement of Agricultural Co-operation in Ireland,* J. G. Knapp. Stationery Office, Dublin, 1964. Commonly known as 'The Knapp Report'.

[8]*The Irish Co-operative Movement* by Patrick Bolger. p. 332, 402.

[9]*The European Recovery Programme – Country Studies: Chapter VIII – Ireland,* Stationery Office Dublin 1948, p. 133. This is a collection of basic documents and background information issued by the Department of External Affairs. The Department also prepared a series of reports for the Oireachtas which were published (also by the Stationery Office) entitled: *The European Recovery Programme, Ireland's Long Term Programme 1949-1953.*

[10]*Irish Agricultural Policies in a Changing World* by I. F. Baillie and S. J. Sheehy. Oliver & Boyd, Edinburgh, 1971. p. 51.

[11]Here I am particularly indebted to the personal recollections of Dr. Louis Smith and to people like Seán Healy and his colleagues in Macra na Feirme and the National Farmers' Association who toured the halls of rural Ireland stressing the need to keep in touch with what was happening on the Continent.

Outside the Debate

[1]See Charles McCarthy *Trade Unions in Ireland, 1894-1960* (Institute of Public Administration, Dublin 1977) for the most exhaustive study made of the Irish Trade Union Movement (Chapters Nine and Ten in particular). There is no reference to either the EEC or EFTA in this monumental work but a good account of the effect of 'the split' on trade union policy towards the E.R.P., pp. 388 and 402.

[2]*Ireland in the Twentieth Century,* by John A. Murphy. Gill & Macmillan, Dublin, 1975.

[3]Northern Ireland Conference of the Irish Trade Union Congress 1958.

[4]*Report on the Possibility of Creating a Free Trade Area,* published by O.E.E.C., Paris, 1957.

[5]Report of the 3rd Annual Conference of the Irish Congress of Trade Unions, July 1961; pp. 262-263.

[6]*The Department's Story: A History of the Department of Agriculture* by D. Hoctor. Institute of Public Administration, Dublin, 1971.

[7]Dáil Éireann. Parliamentary Debates. Vol. 163, col. 651.

[8]*Administration,* 1957-8, pp. 25-42.

[9]*Report of Public Services Organisation Review Group 1966-1969,* par. 3.1.11.

[10]*Economic Development.* Stationery Office. Dublin 1958. Pr. 4803.

[11]*The Irish Civil Service* by Seán Dooney. Institute of Public Administration Dublin, 1976; pp. 5 and 7.

[12]Recollections of Dr. T. Ó Raifeartaigh, former Secretary of the Department of Education who, as Assistant Secretary, attended many of the meetings from 1950 onwards on behalf of the Department – Interview given 10 January, 1978.

[13]*The Irish Department of Finance 1922-1958* by Ronan Fanning. Institute of Public Administration, Dublin 1978, p.411.

[14]Note of discussion at Treasury 21 June, 1948, F. 17/6/58. See Fanning *op. cit* p. 427.

[15]Department of Finance Files: 31 July 1951. See Fanning p. 489.

[16]Finance Files: 23 June 1953. Fanning pp. 489-90.

[17]*Administration,* 2, 3, pp. 61-68.

[18]*Administration,* 9, 1, p. 83.

[19]A senior civil servant in a personal memorandum to the author.

[20]*From Protection to Free Trade.* Text of Seán Lemass Memorial Lecture delivered at the University of Exeter, 17 January 1974 by T. K. Whitaker and published *Administration* Winter 1973.

[21]Statements made by M. J. Haughey, chairman, C.T.T., in the course of his Annual Report. Copy in files of Córas Tráchtála.

The Verdict

[1]*Europe in Question – Theories of Regional Integration* by R. J. Harrison. George Allen and Unwin Ltd., London 1974. pp. 247 and 248.

[2]*Limits and Problems of European Integration* Stichting Grotius Seminarium. Conference of May 30 – June 2, 1961. Nijhoff, The Hague, 1963; p. 2.

Bibliography

Files, documents and internal newsletters of organisations:

Comhairle le Leas Óige – File relating to European Youth Campaign (unclassified).

Council of Europe – File relating to Ireland; Historical Archives of Council of Europe, Strasbourg; File No. 789/0212.

European Movement – Files; Archives of College of Europe, Bruges (unclassified).

European Movement – Files; Headquarters of International European Movement, Brussels (unclassified).

European Youth Campaign – Files; Archives of College of Europe, Bruges (unclassified).

Irish Association of Catholic University Students – Newsletters (temporarily in custody of author).

Irish Council of European Movement – Files; European, Dublin (unclassified).

Official publications:

An Appraisement of Agricultural Co-operation in Ireland. Report by J. G. Knapp, Stationery Office, Dublin, 1964.

Bunreacht na hÉireann (The Constitution of Ireland).

Censorship of Publications Act, 1929 (Amended 1964).

Dáil Reports.

Official *Reports* of the Council of Europe.

Programme for Economic Expansion. November 1958.

Report of Commission appointed in 1948 to study 'Irish Population Problems'. ISO, July 1954.

Report on the Possibility of Creating a Free Trade Area.OEEC, Paris 1957.

The European Economic Community, White Paper, June 1961.

The European Recovery Programme. Stationery Office, Dublin 1948.

Treaty of the European Coal and Steel Community.

Treaty of the European Community for Atomic Energy.

Treaty of the European Economic Community.

Ulster Year Books. Published: H.M. Stationery Office.

Yearbook of European Convention of Human Rights: IV.

Newspapers, periodicals, pamphlets, reports and handbooks:
Administration.
Comhar.
Commentary. Publication of EYC in Ireland.
Éire/Ireland. Weekly Bulletin of the Department of External Affairs. Published for dissemination through Irish missions abroad.
European Monetary Union and the Sterling Link. Pamphlet: Published Irish Council of the European Movement, 1975.
European Youth Campaign in Ireland. Published: EYC, Dublin 1954.
Institute of Bankers in Ireland – Journal of.
Irish Farmers Journal.
Irish Post.
Irish Review and Annual (1959, 1960, 1961). *The Irish Times.*
Irish Woman (Official publication of Irish Countrywomen's Association).
Methodes et Mouvements pour Unir l'Europe. Bulletin de la Centre Europeenne de la Culture, Geneva. May 1958.
Muintir na Tíre Guide. Published 1958.
Muintir na Tíre Handbook. Published 1941.
Procedure of the Consultative Assembly. Published by the Council of Europe, Strasbourg 1953.
Radio Telefís Éireann – *First Annual Report.* March 1961.
Regeneration – Rural Resurgence in Ireland. Irish Farmers' Association, 1975.
Social Security: Outlines of a Scheme of National Health Insurance by Dr Dignam, Bishop of Clonfert, 1944.
Studies.
The European Teacher. Published: Irish Section of the European Association of Teachers.
The Federation of Irish Manufacturers – *Annual Reports* of.
Irish Independent.
The Irish Press.
The Irish Times.
The Leader.
The Nation. 1 March 1848.
The Spectator.
The Statist.
The Union of Europe. Published by the American Committee on United Europe, in co-operation with the European Movement, 1950.
Towards a European Government. Henri Brugmans. Published: EYC, Paris 1953.
Tribute to a Great European – J. H. Retinger. Centre Europeenne de la Culture. n.d.

Recordings and publicity material on radio broadcasts:

Recordings of highlights of the year on discs, classified under the year in question, for most of the 1950s. These discs may soon be transposed onto tape.

Daybooks for each year with varying amount of detail on the content of programmes which were broadcast.

Published works:

Anon. *Limits and Problems of European Integration* – Stichtung Grotius Seminarium – Conference of May 30-June 2, 1961. Martinus Nijhoff, The Hague, 1963.

Armstrong, John A. *The European Administrative Elite*. Princeton University Press, 1973.

Baillie, I. F. and S. J. Sheehy. *Irish Agricultural Policies in a Changing World*. Oliver & Boyd, Edinburgh, 1971.

Beever, R. Colin. *European Unity and the Trade Union Movement*. A. W. Sythoff, Leyden, 1960.

Bolger, Patrick. *The Irish Co-operative Movement – Its History and Development*. Institute of Public Administration, Dublin, 1977.

Cohan, Al. *The Irish Political Elite*. *Studies in Irish Political Culture 4*. Gill & Macmillan, Dublin, 1972.

Crawley, Aidan. *De Gaulle*. A Biography. London, 1969.

de Gaulle, Charles. *Memoirs d'Éspoir*. Le Renouveau 1962-1970. Plon, Paris, 1970.

Deutsch, Karl. *The Analysis of International Relations*. Prentice-Hall, 1968.

Digby, Margaret. *The World Co-operative Movement*. Hutchinson's University Library, London, 1948.

Doolan, Lelia, Jack Dowling and Bob Quinn. *Sit Down and Be Counted – The Cultural Evolution of a Television Station*. Wellington Publishers Ltd., Dublin, 1969.

Dooney, Seán. *The Irish Civil Service*. Institute of Public Administration, Dublin, 1976.

Dwyer, T. Ryle. *Irish Neutrality and the U.S.A. 1939-1945*. Gill & Macmillan, Dublin, 1977.

Edwards, R. Dudley. *A New History of Ireland*. Gill & Macmillan, Dublin, 1972.

Ellis, P. Beresford. *A History of the Irish Working Class*. Gollancz, London, 1972.

Einzig, Paul. *The Case Against Joining the Common Market*. Macmillan & Co., London, 1971.

Fanning, Ronan. *The Irish Department of Finance 1922-1958*. Institute of Public Administration, Dublin, 1978.

FitzGerald, Garret. *State-Sponsored Bodies*. Institute of Public Administration, Dublin, 1963.

Gibson, Norman J. and John E. Spencer (Eds.). *Economic Activity in Ireland – A Study of Two Open Economies*. Gill & Macmillan, Dublin, 1977.

Gorham, Maurice. *Forty Years of Irish Broadcasting*. Talbot Press, Dublin, 1965.

Haas, Ernst. *International Political Communities*. Anchor Books, 1966.

Harrison, R. J. *Europe in Question*. Allen & Unwin, London, 1974.

Hillary, Brian, Aidan Kelly and A. I. Marsh. *Trade Union Organisation in Ireland*. Irish Productivity Centre, Dublin, 1975.

Hoctor, D. *The Department's Story: A History of the Department of Agriculture*. Institute of Public Administration, Dublin, 1971.

Hodges, (Ed.). *European Integration*. Penguin, 1972.

Ionescu, Ghita (Ed.). *The New Politics of European Integration*. Macmillan: St. Martin's Press, London, 1972.

Keatinge, Patrick. *A Place Among the Nations – Issues of Irish Foreign Policy*. Institute of Public Administration, Dublin, 1978.

The Formulation of Irish Foreign Policy. Institute of Public Administration, Dublin, 1973.

Kelly, J. M. *Fundamental Rights in the Irish Law and Constitution*. Allen Figgis & Co., Dublin, 1961.

Kendall, Walter. *The Labour Movement in Europe*. Allen Lane, London, 1975.

Kennedy, Kieran A. and Brendan R. Dowling. *Economic Growth in Ireland – The Experience Since 1947*. Gill & Macmillan in association with The Economic & Social Research Institute, Dublin, 1975.

Knapp, J. G. *An Appraisement of Agricultural Co-operation in Ireland*. Stationery Office, Dublin, 1964.

Longford, The Earl of, and Thomas P. O'Neill. *Eamon de Valera*. Gill & Macmillan, Dublin, 1970.

Lyons, F. S. L. *Ireland Since the Famine*. Collins/Fontana, Second Edition, 1972.

McCarthy, Charles. *Trade Unions in Ireland, 1894-1960*. Institute of Public Administration, Dublin, 1977.

Manning, Maurice. *Irish Political Parties*. Gill & Macmillan, Dublin, 1972.

Marriott, J. A. R. *Federalism and the Small State*. Allen & Unwin, London, 1943.

Mayne, Richard. *Recovery of Europe: From Destruction to Unity*. Weidenfeld & Nicholson, London, 1970.

Meenan, James. *The Irish Economy Since 1922*. Liverpool University Press, 1970.

Miljan, Toivo. *The Reluctant Europeans – The Attitudes of the Nordic Countries Towards European Integration*. C. Hurst & Co., London, 1977.

Mitrany, David. *A Working Peace System*. Quadrangle Books, Chicago, 1966.

Moody, T. W. and F. X. Martin (Eds.). *The Course of Irish History*. Mercier Press, Cork, 1967.

Mowatt, R. C. *Creating the European Community*. Blandford Press, London, 1973.

Moynihan, Maurice. *Currency and Central Banking in Ireland 1922-1960.*Gill & Macmillan in association with the Central Bank of Ireland, Dublin, 1975.

Murphy, John A. *Ireland in the Twentieth Century*. Gill & Macmillan, 1975.

Newman, Jeremiah. *The Future of Rural Ireland*. The Talbot Press, Dublin, 1958.

Nowlan, Kevin B. and T. Desmond Williams (Eds.). *Ireland in the War Years and After – 1939-1951*. Macmillan, 1969.

O'Brien, Conor Cruise. *To Katanga and Back – A U.N. Case History*. Hutchinson, London, 1962.

O'Neill, Terence. *Ulster at the Crossroads*. Faber & Faber, London, 1969.

Pomian, John (Ed.). *Joseph Retinger – Memoirs of an Eminence Grise*. Sussex University Press, 1972.

Powell, Enoch. *The Common Market – The Case Against*. Elliott Right Way Books, London, 1972.

Pryce, Roy. *The Politics of the European Community*. Butterworths, London and Boston, 1973.

Raven, John, C. T. Whelan et al. *Political Culture in Ireland: The Views of Two Generations*. Institute of Public Administration, Dublin, 1976.

Tait, A. A. and J. A. Bristow. *Ireland: Some Problems of a Developing Economy*. Gill & Macmillan, Dublin, 1972.

Thomas, Hugh. *Europe – The Radical Challenge*. Weidenfeld & Nicholson, London, 1973.

Toner, Jerome, O.P. *Rural Ireland – Some of Its Problems*. Clonmore & Reynolds, Dublin, 1955.

Vaizey, John (Ed.) *Economic Sovereignty and Regional Policy – A Symposium on Regional Policy in Britain and Ireland*. Gill & Macmillan, Dublin, 1975.

Whyte, J. H. *Church and State in Modern Ireland – 1923-1970*. Gill & Macmillan, Dublin, 1971.

Index